A Plymouth Pilgrim

**WILLIAM BRADFORD'S EYEWITNESS
ACCOUNT OF THE MAYFLOWER PASSENGERS**

*THOROUGHLY MODERNIZED
FOR TODAY'S READERS*

*"I shall now unfold the circumstances,
motives, and simple truth
of our story from the very beginning,
in plain language,
as best as I can remember."*

William Bradford

The official seventeenth-century seal of Plymouth Plantation of Massachusetts.

A Plymouth Pilgrim

WILLIAM BRADFORD'S EYEWITNESS
ACCOUNT OF THE MAYFLOWER PASSENGERS

ADAPTED AND ILLUSTRATED

BY

DONALD W. WHITE

A Plymouth Pilgrim:
William Bradford's Eyewitness Account
of the Mayflower Passengers

First Printing

Copyright © 2015 by Donald W. White

All rights reserved.

The original, unedited text by William Bradford is in the public domain. However, no part of this publication may be reproduced or electronically stored without explicit permission of the author.

Printed in the United States of America
ISBN: 978-1480225497

Cover photo by Joseph Sohm,
© Americanspirit | Dreamstime.com

Author's website at:
www.donaldwaynewhite.com

To my family,
and especially my father
who gave to me a
love for American history.

I also express gratitude to the good
people at the living museums of:

Plimoth Plantation
Wampanoag Homesite
Mayflower II

for all their hard work, attention to detail,
and their passion to bring the rest of us
back in time 400 years.

CONTENTS

Preface ix
Introduction xi

1. **Losing Our Liberties:** 1
   Why We Must Leave

2. **Escape to Holland:** 8
   The Struggle to Be Free

3. **Life in Leiden:** 14
   Community and Controversy

4. **Time to Leave:** 20
   Freedoms and Risks in Holland

5. **Dreams of America:** 26
   Our Difficult and Dangerous Decision

6. **Negotiations:** 44
   Our Dealings with Greed and Grievance

7. **Saying Goodbye:** 66
   Hearts Break as We Sail

8. **Our Journey Delays:** 78
   Sabotage and Endless Repairs

9.	**Dangerous Crossing:** Our Two Months at Sea	86
10.	**Finding a Home:** The Search for a Place to Settle	93
11.	**The Sickness:** How Half Our Number Died	104
12.	**Springtime to Harvest:** Surviving Our First Year	117

APPENDICES:

1.	Bradford's Victory Sermon	130
2.	Mayflower Passengers and Families	134
3.	Timeline of Events Leading to Plymouth	139
4.	Sampling of Bradford's Original Writing	145
	Recommended Resources	148

PREFACE

WHAT DOES IT MEAN to be an American? How can people of different faiths and cultures live together in peace? Are individual rights more important than the common good? Why do droves of immigrants risk their lives in pilgrimages to America?

These are some of today's most crucial American questions and they are at the very heart of the 400-year-old Plymouth Pilgrim story, making the real-life adventure of 102 English settlers even more important today.

William Bradford, one of the original *Mayflower* passengers and the most influential leader of the Plymouth Colony in Massachusetts, wrote an extensive firsthand account of the Pilgrims' story, however the language is so archaic (see Appendix 4) as to make it nearly impossible for modern readers to understand.

The book you are now reading is a radically updated version of Bradford's own story, paraphrased so as to sound as if Governor Bradford is sitting near your fireplace, sharing his gripping story with you over hot tea and biscuits.

This is the true story of the Plymouth Pilgrims—the uniquely American story of hope and tragedy that is discussed in every American classroom and annually celebrated in nearly every American home. The year 2020 marks the 400th anniversary (quadricentennial) of the *Mayflower* landing, so now is a good time to read the dramatic true story as told by Governor William Bradford, the faithful and careworn leader of the Plymouth Pilgrims.

INTRODUCTION

GOVERNOR BRADFORD'S MASSIVE original volume recounts the first twenty-six years of Plymouth Plantation, however this book concludes just one year after the famous landing at Cape Cod, covering all the events that fascinate us most, from their religious persecution in England and European exile, to the *Mayflower*'s transatlantic journey, their first encounters with Native Americans, and the triumphal harvest celebration that we now call the "First Thanksgiving."

If you are interested in the roots of American history, this little book is the clearest reading yet of the Pilgrims' own story, with all of their seventeenth century religious and European biases. The Pilgrims are neither demonized nor idolized. This is Bradford's own story on his terms, but updated for twenty-first century readers so that you can clearly grasp their challenges, their frustrations, their fears and faith, and be swept up in their compelling true adventure. My design is not to change the voice of the storyteller, but to make his voice as clear as possible, allowing their drama to unfold while remaining faithful to the spirit and content of his original account.

Bradford's language is updated and condensed, but the original chronology and chapter divisions remain so you can read this book alongside older editions. Chapters eleven and twelve in *this* book correspond to the first two chapters of *Book II* in the original. If you are reading Bradford's original text, you can use this book to clarify his many tedious and confusing passages.

Wherever appropriate, I have changed Bradford's third person narrative to first person, making a dry historical record come alive as the captivating firsthand experience that it truly is. Enigmatic references to obscure people, places, events, and beliefs are all clearly revealed in the text itself as integral parts of the story so the reader is not distracted by footnotes and puzzling historical references, but can read this 400-year-old story as easily as any modern day novel. The only footnotes included are Bradford's literary and biblical references. Bradford himself cited most of his references, but I've noted other citations where they were clearly identifiable.

This book is not meant to replace larger, authoritative editions of Bradford's journal, but many will never read those editions because of their size and dated language. However, this should be an ideal introduction to Pilgrim studies, or a guide to help you understand Bradford's writings, or perhaps just an enjoyable version for those who want to read Bradford's own eyewitness account of the Pilgrims.

Before you read on, let's address some common misconceptions. Did the Pilgrims belong to the English Puritan movement? Yes—and no. You would have difficulty finding any differences in their beliefs, but the main distinction is that the Pilgrims gave up all hope of "purifying" the Church of England from "Catholic influences." In separating themselves from the official state church, the Pilgrims are more accurately called "Separatists."

Did the *Mayflower* passengers sail to America for religious freedom? Yes—and no. Just over one third of the 102 settlers (including Bradford) were fleeing the religious constraints they suffered in England. The rest, however, sailed to New England to find fortune, adventure, or perhaps relief from overpopulated English cities. Bradford calls these people "strangers."

At the end of each chapter are questions for students, reading groups, or personal reflection to help you connect these historical events to our issues today and hopefully bring you closer to the brave adventurers whose tragic stories have become so dear to us all.

Thank you, dear readers, for joining me on this adventure. Prepare yourselves for the frustrations and trepidations, the tragedies and triumphs of the people that we call "the Pilgrims."

Donald W. White

CHAPTER 1

Losing Our Liberty

Why We must Leave

THIS WE ALL KNOW—Satan has continued to war against God's people in England, and it has been happening ever since the true Christian gospel burst forth in our beloved nation.

Ours was the first nation the Lord adorned with that True Light since the darkness of Catholicism covered the Christian world. Bloody deaths, torture, prison, and banishment have been Satan's tactics for fear his kingdom would fail and truth prevail as churches of God return to their ancient purity, order, liberty, and beauty.

Since he could not prevail against the gospel in the earliest times, as it quickly took root around the world, watered by the blood of martyrs, Satan chose an ancient strategy—heresy. And with it came its woeful effects of bitter contention, confusion, division, vile ceremonies, and useless decrees. Eventually the persecutions that Christians inflicted upon one another became no different from that of unbelievers. The true Christians were also forced to contend with corrupt heretics, such as the Arians who cast doubt upon the divinity of Christ.

In his history of the ancient church, Socrates Scholasticus said, "Their violence was truly no less than that of those who had formerly compelled the Christians to sacrifice to idols. For many of them endured all kinds of scourgings, a variety of tortures," such as the rack and dismemberment, "and confiscation of their property. Many were punished with exile; some died under the torturers and others were put to death as they were banished into exile" never to see their country again.[1]

After the Antichrist ("that man of sin"[2]) corrupted the church, the truth had finally burst forth, but ever since then Satan has used the same torments today.

When that ancient serpent couldn't prevail by flames of cruel torture, he fought with flames of contention, destroying the kingdom and doctrines of Christ by bringing discord between the Christian reformers themselves.

In his *Book of Martyrs*, John Foxe reveals how the faithful were tormented and burned under Queen Mary's rule. To escape that cruelty, nearly 800 English Christians fled to the European cities of Wesel, Frankfurt, Basel, Emden, Marburg, Strasburg, and Geneva. After fleeing, many had found themselves still persecuted for their refusal to abide by the ceremonies, service books, and other Catholic practices that still plague England like the

---

[1] Socrates Scholasticus, *Ecclesiastical Hist.*, Vol 2, Ch 27 (c. 439).
[2] 2Thessalonians 2:3.

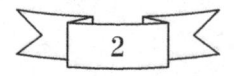

ancient idolatrous sites that were the scorn of the biblical prophets and the ruination of Israel. Even in Frankfurt, Englishmen not only continued their unbiblical practices, but they even defended them as Mr. Whittingham tells us in his book, which everyone should know and consider.[3]

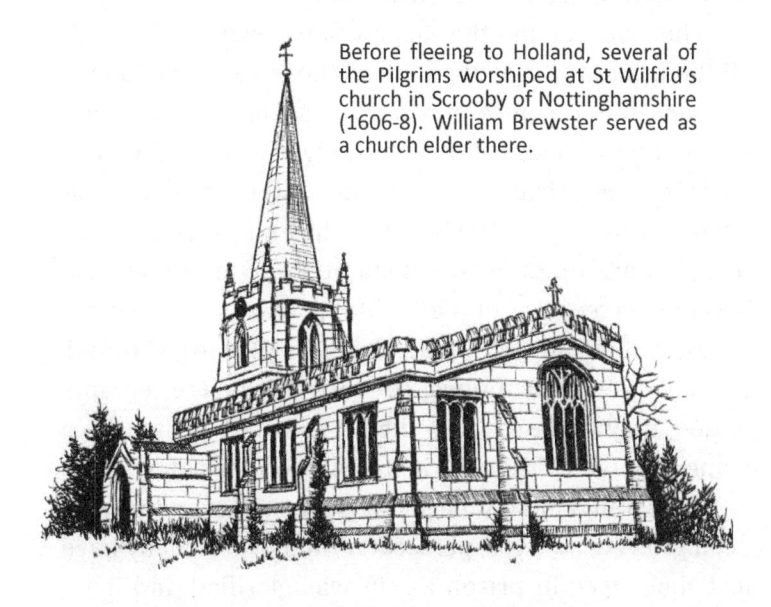

Before fleeing to Holland, several of the Pilgrims worshiped at St Wilfrid's church in Scrooby of Nottinghamshire (1606-8). William Brewster served as a church elder there.

Some of us had merely desired proper worship, godly living, and to choose our own church leaders according to the purity of the Scriptures, without the inventions of men. Others, however, sought greatness in the church by power, seeking the worldly trappings of high office. No one, not even that great reformer John Calvin, could sway

---

[3] William Whittingham, *A Brief Discourse of the Troubles at Frankfurt* (1575).

them from their tyranny as they persecuted the servants of God, charging them with rebellion and treason.

When Queen Mary died, many Christian exiles returned to England under a gracious Queen Elizabeth, only to find that others turned her against the faithful, declaring them as dangerous to the nation.

The ignorant and the superstitious desperately needed the basics of Christian faith in those days. We longed to teach them a pure and harmless Christian practice, reforming the church, but apparently it was not the time. False teachers charmed even some of the godly into following their popish trash (which has no basis in Scripture, but are relics of "that man of sin"[4]) until they also became persecutors of the faithful in our land. The more the light of the gospel spread, the more they urged others to follow their corruptions. To mock the sincere servants of God, they imposed upon them the name "Puritans"—a name adopted by the self-righteous Novatians of old.[5]

True religion has been disgraced. The godly have been grieved, afflicted, persecuted, and exiled. Many have lost their lives in prison as sin was glorified and ignorance, corruption, and atheism increased, and the papists are therefore encouraged to hope another day.

This is what moved William Perkins, that holy man of Cambridge University, to cry out in his powerful preaching on repentance from Zephaniah 2:1-2. He said that,

---

[4] 2Thessalonians 2:3.
[5] Jerome, *Lives of Illustrious Men,* Ch 70 (c. 393).

True religion has been with us for thirty-five years, but the more it is preached, the more it is condemned and mocked by many. Instead of scoffing at corruption and wickedness, religion itself is now a joke, a laughingstock and a target of reproach, so that in England these days the men and women who profess true religion and wish to serve God must prepare to sustain mockery and injury just as if they lived among the enemies of the faith![6]

Though many were enlightened by the word of God and the work of godly preachers, they were immediately scoffed at and scorned by the profane multitude. Ministers were urged to fall in line or be silenced. For years the people bore with patience the torments of church officials. From the light of God's Word they came to realize that they should not bow down to the tyrannous powers of church officials, those who profane the worship of God by adding unlawful fabrications to Christian faith and practice—things that are used in Catholic popery.

A Dutch historian says that when King James began his rule, "he found that the now reformed Church of England was still much like the reformed church in the days of King Edward VI. They continued to keep the spiritual position of the bishops just as in the old days. This is very different from the reformed churches of Scotland, France, the Netherlands, Emden, and Geneva," whose reformed religion in those places seems much more like the very

---

[6] William Perkins, "A Warning against the Idolatry of the Last Times" (1601).

first Christian churches from the days of the Apostles.[7]

Many saw the evil of these religious practices and shook off the burden of anti-Christian bondage. As the Lord's free people, they made a covenant to join together as a church family to walk in the way of the Lord whatever the cost and, as this journal will show, there was indeed a cost.

These people became two distinct church bodies among several towns and villages, some in Nottinghamshire, Lincolnshire, and Yorkshire. One church, led by the gifted preacher John Smith, left the truth for falsehood. The other church was led by worthy men such as Richard Clifton, John Robinson, and William Brewster.

This is the church of which I must write. This is the church which gave birth to Plymouth Plantation. This is our story.

Our peace in England was short-lived. We were hunted and persecuted on every side. The earlier afflictions were fleabites compared to what we later faced. Some were thrown in prison. Others had their homes surrounded, watched day and night, barely escaping. Yet we expected all of this, and we endured these afflictions by the help of God. However, after unceasing and unbending persecution, most of us were compelled to leave our homes and livelihood behind, fleeing to the Netherlands where we heard that people enjoyed religious freedom. So in the year 1607 we resolved to leave for Holland.

---

[7] Emanuel van Meteren, *The General History of the Netherlands*, Vol 25 (c. 1608).

QUESTIONS FOR REFLECTION AND DISCUSSION:

1. Why might William Bradford begin his book with a short history of religious persecution?

2. According to this chapter, why is Bradford's Christian group at odds with the authorities?

3. Bradford identifies what he sees as various devilish tactics against the church. What are they?

4. How did Bradford's people react to religious persecution?

5. Compare how he describes the church authorities of his day with his own church group.

6. What are the greatest challenges regarding religious biases today?

CHAPTER 2

Escape to Holland

The Struggle to Be Free
1607 - 1608

LEAVING OUR HOMELAND, our friends, our family is difficult enough. But to enter a strange country, whose language we did not know, uncertain as to how we would live—this was a desperate, intolerable misery. As farmers, we were not acquainted with Holland's economy built upon trade and commerce. However, we were not dismayed by the challenge before us. We placed our trust in God and decided to leave.

As a persecuted people, we could no longer stay in England, but nor were we allowed to go. All the ports and harbors were closed to us. We had no choice but to travel in secret, paying bribes and extraordinary rates to gain passage. Even so, we were often betrayed; our people and our possessions were captured by the government.

We created a plan for many of us to sail out from Boston in the eastern county of Lincolnshire. We paid a large sum for the exclusive use of a ship, arranging a secret departure time with the captain.

That day arrived. We waited anxious hours, the time long past. At nighttime the ship finally sailed in. We quickly loaded ourselves and our goods. However, once we were all safely aboard the ship, we were seized. The captain betrayed us into the hands of the authorities.

The officers searched us, ransacked our possessions, and even searched our women in an improper manner. They marched us back into town, making a spectacle of us before onlookers. They stripped us of our money, our books, and other goods.

They brought us before the magistrates, who gave us what leeway they could, but they could not release us without an order from the council. They kept us in prison an entire month before finally allowing us to return home. Seven of us, however, were held over for trial.

Spring arrived, and even more joined our group for another attempt to flee England. We met in secret with a Dutch ship captain. We explained our situation, hoping to find him more trustworthy than that captain from our own country, and the Dutchman assured us. He would pick us up between the towns of Grimsby and Hull in a large open field, far from any village. Our women, children, and supplies would be sent there in a small ship at the appointed time. The men would all arrive on foot.

When the time came, the women and children all anxiously awaited aboard the little English ship, while the Dutchman's ship was scheduled to arrive the next day.

Then the sea began to churn and our women grew sick. They asked the crew to put in at a nearby creek, but when they did the ship ran aground. The tide was too low.

The Dutchman and his crew arrived the next morning and found the little ship and all its passengers still grounded in the midst of the creek. There was no hope of budging it until the water rose again at noon. As they waited for high tide, the Dutch captain put down a small boat to begin retrieving the men waiting upon the shore.

Many of us had safely boarded the ship, and the boat was just about to retrieve more men, when the captain spied a large crowd quickly approaching. They came on foot and on horseback, armed with guns and other weapons. It seemed the whole countryside was hastening out to capture us.

With the wind blowing, the Dutchman cursed under his breath and ordered his crew to pull up anchor and head out. As we began to pull away, we watched our wives and children stranded aboard that tiny ship at the mercy of an angry, gathering crowd. We would have given anything to be with our loved ones, but we could do nothing. In tears, we sailed away with only the clothes on our backs and scarcely a penny among us, for all we owned was on that small now-captured English vessel.

At least fourteen days we were at sea. For seven of those days the skies were so dark that we saw no sun, no moon, not one star. A treacherous storm surged up, pushing us north toward Norway. Even the sailors feared for their lives. In the worst of the storm the crewmen gave up all hope, crying and shrieking that we were all about to sink.

But even as the sea filled our mouths and ears, we cried out to the Lord in passionate prayer. While the crew shouted, "We are sinking! We are sinking!" our men cried out in faith, "But you can save us, Lord! You can save us!" It was then by the Lord's mercy and power that the ship began to right herself and the storm began to calm. The courage of the crew returned, and the Lord gave us a peace that passes all understanding.[8] We reached our chosen harbor where the people came flocking, amazed at our deliverance, for the storm was so long and fierce.

Of those poor men left upon the English shore as the armed crowds came, those who were in the greatest danger from the authorities managed to escape. Others, however, were unwilling to leave the women who were still stranded offshore on that little ship. It was a pitiful sight for those men to see the women shivering in the cold, all of them weeping, some for their frightened children and others for the uncertain fate of their husbands on the fleeing Dutch ship.

Those who were left behind were captured, taken from one place to another and one judge to another. The officials didn't know what to do with them, for it seemed unreasonable to imprison so many women and children whose only crime was their desire to be with their husbands and fathers. However, sending them home was just

---

[8] Philippians 4:7.

as difficult for they had no home. We all sold our homes just before our planned journey. Eventually, after they were thoroughly harassed and taken from one officer to another, the authorities were content to release them and finally be rid of them.

Though I cannot write about all the troubles we endured as we tried to flee, I must tell about the fruit of our efforts. Our cause became famous and moved many others to consider it themselves. Our Christian behavior left a deep impression in their minds and gave others courage to follow our path.

In the end, despite the storms of opposition, one way or another we all finally arrived in Holland with no small rejoicing.

QUESTIONS FOR REFLECTION AND DISCUSSION:

1. Is it ever in the best interest of a nation to suppress religious freedom? Explain.

2. What kinds of circumstances would it take to force you and your family to flee to a strange and unfamiliar place?

3. What people groups do you know who are unnecessarily harassed by authorities, and what is your responsibility toward them?

4. The Dutch ship managed to help *some* men escape to Holland, while leaving many behind. Put yourself in the place of those men who were left onshore as the mobs approached, or the women who were helplessly stuck on the English ship. How would you manage to cope?

5. Bradford describes a near wreck of the fleeing Dutch ship in which even the experienced sailors feared for their lives. How would such a terrifyingly close call with death impact your life?

CHAPTER 3

Life in Leiden

Community and Controversy
1609 - 1620

IN HOLLAND THERE WERE many large fortified cities. We were exposed to strange customs, fashions, and language, but the strangeness of the country was not our main concern. Amidst the wealth of our new home, we saw the grim face of poverty coming upon us like an armed and dangerous man.[9] However, we were armed with faith and patience, and by the help of God we prevailed.

Pastor Robinson, Mr. Brewster, and other leaders finally joined us in Holland, and we reexamined our living situation and church affairs. By that time we had lived in Amsterdam about a year. John Robinson and others saw how Pastor John Smith (our friend from Lincolnshire)

---

[9] Proverbs 24:34.

and his followers were already deep in doctrinal controversies with the established church in Amsterdam, and we knew that we ourselves could not fix the problem. We decided it was best to move away before our people were also caught up in the conflicts.

We chose the beautiful city of Leiden. Though it was famous for its university, it lacked the employment opportunities of coastal Amsterdam. We did the best we could, however, treasuring peace and spiritual comfort over any worldly wealth. And over time, with hard work, we made a satisfactory living.

We continued many comfortable years in Leiden under the able leadership of Pastor John Robinson and his assistant, Elder William Brewster. We grew in the knowledge and graces of God, living together in peace and holiness. Many more came from different parts of England, increasing the size of our congregation. We quickly dealt with any differences or quarrels that arose, so that love and peace continued. In a few rare cases, after every possible solution failed, we had to purge the church of those who refused to work together.

There was such a strong mutual love between our church and Pastor Robinson that it was difficult to tell who was more delighted: him or the people. He loved us deeply and sought our greatest good, both body and soul. He was a capable leader in both spiritual and civil affairs. He could foresee any potential struggles and looked after our physical welfare just as a father for his children.

There were three kinds of people who angered the pastor most, however: those who isolated themselves from others, rigid people who criticized others' faults while ignoring their own, and those whose conversations were less than virtuous. Yet even these people held our pastor in high regard, respecting him while he was alive, and mourning his loss when he died years later. What a treasure he was. His death left a wound that never

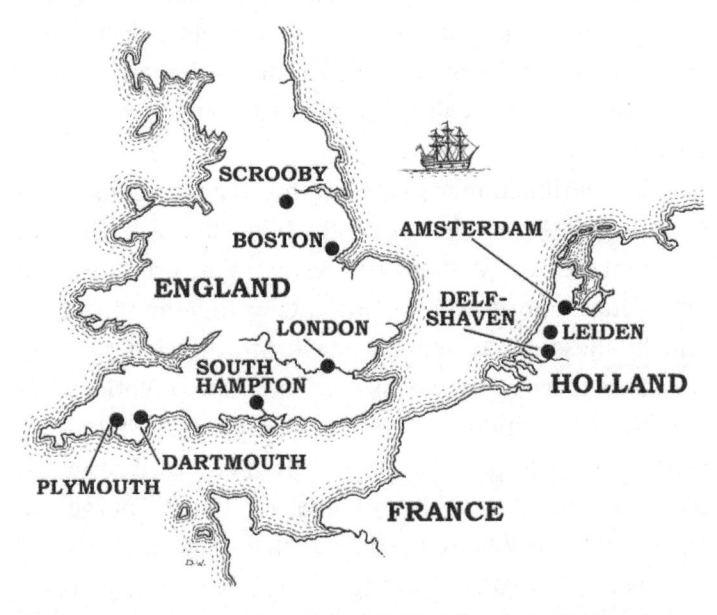

healed. But in those wonderful days back in Holland, our congregation had such love for God and for one another that we came as close to the ancient pattern of the biblical church as any church today has ever done.

I will not recount all our experiences in Holland, for that would be an entire book, but I will reveal to you the roots of what became our settlement at New Plymouth.

Years later, after we left Holland, some antagonists

slanderously claimed that Dutch officials drove us out. Nothing was further from the truth! In ancient times godless historians told the same lies of Moses and the Israelites when they left Egypt. Our people had a wonderful relationship with the Dutch and a good reputation among them. Even when we were initially poor, their bakers and merchants would still extend credit to us because they knew that we kept our word. Employers sought us out because of our honesty and hard work.

Leiden's city officials praised our people even as they rebuked a local French-speaking church, telling them, "These English people have lived with us for twelve years now and they have never given us a reason to complain, however your strifes and quarrels are continual!"

Religious Controversies

In those days there was great theological controversy in Holland due to the followers of Jacobus Arminius, who taught that one may willfully refuse the Lord's grace and forgiveness. He formerly taught in the University of Leiden, so there were daily disputes there among students and scholars, especially between the professors Simon Episcopius and Johannes Polyander. Neither of their followers would even listen to the other professor teach.

Though our Pastor Robinson was busy with his own writing and teaching in the church, he daily attended the lectures of both professors. He became so well acquainted with their arguments and tactics that no one else was more capable of debating the issues. Professor Polyander himself, along with Leiden's foremost preachers, pleaded with Pastor Robinson to debate Mr. Episcopius. But because Mr. Robinson was a foreigner in Leiden, he was reluctant to get involved. We persisted, however, telling him that if he did not help us fight against the heretical teachings of Jacobus Arminius, then the truth itself would suffer at the hands of our persuasive adversary, Mr. Episcopius.

Our pastor agreed and so prepared to defend the truth in public debate. With the Lord's help, when that day came Pastor Robinson defeated our adversary, baffling him before the public. Mr. Robinson was such a formidable threat that Professor Episcopius was forced to prepare all the more diligently for their debates. Two or three times our pastor brought such public victory to the truth, moving many to praise God, winning the respect of scholars and truth-lovers alike.

Far from being tired of our people, the Dutch in fact wanted us to stay if only it would not anger the English authorities. In fact when we began to consider moving to America, prominent citizens of Leiden made generous offers to keep us there.

I could share many such examples, exposing the lies of those who claim we were forced out of Holland. These will suffice, however, for only a few believed those hateful, disgraceful rumors.

QUESTIONS FOR REFLECTION AND DISCUSSION:

1. Describe their struggles as exiles in Holland.

2. How did religious disagreements impact the lives of Pastor John Robinson and his followers?

3. How does Bradford describe their church's relationship with the Dutch? How does that compare with the rumors that circulated about their church?

4. What does Bradford have to say about Pastor John Robinson? Who do you personally know who is a spiritual or moral leader to you or others?

5. Explain Bradford's attitude about religious conflicts.

6. What are the best ways to deal with religious or philosophical disagreements today?

CHAPTER 4

Time to Leave

Freedoms and Risks in Holland
1609 - 1620

WE LIVED IN LEIDEN some eleven or twelve years, during the truce between the Netherlands and Spain. In those years some of our congregation died and many others grew old. With lessons learned from experience, our leaders began to see some dangers in our present circumstances, so they reconsidered our plans for the future. After much serious discussion we all decided it was time to find a new home.

Despite the religious freedom in Holland, life was oppressively harsh. Just as Orpah tearfully left Naomi,[10] so too many of our people returned to England in tearful reluctance because life in Leiden was just so difficult. To them it was better to live under the constant threat of

---

[10] Ruth 1:14.

jail, being persecuted for their faith, than remain in Leiden under such painful hardship. Pastor Robinson said that if there was a place for us to live with both freedom and comfort, then even our critics would join us.

Secondly, though we gladly endured hardships when we were young and strong, old age crept upon many of us, and all the more quickly by the hard labor. We could be crushed by our burdens within just a few years.

Like cautious warriors, we also realized the possibility that our enemies might sneak into Leiden and seize us, leaving us unable to flee or defend ourselves. As the divine proverb says, "A prudent man foresees the evil and hides himself,"[11] so we thought it best to find a home with fewer such risks.

We ourselves were nearly becoming slave-drivers, not only to our servants, but even to our dear children, breaking the hearts of their parents. In Leiden even the most obedient children, trained to work hard from an early age, found their young bodies weakening and aging under the burdens of labor.

The worst sorrow, however, was that our own children were enticed by the temptations of that place, becoming like the Dutch in their language, culture, and life. Many saw the unrestrained immorality around them and they were lured far away from the godly lives of their parents. Some chose to become soldiers, sailors, or even worse, endangering their souls, grieving their parents, and dishonoring the Lord. If we had remained in Holland,

---

[11] Proverbs 22:3.

our future generations would be in grave danger of complete corruption.

Lastly, there was within us a burning desire to spread the gospel of Christ to the distant parts of the world, or at least be the stepping stones for others to do so. For these reasons and more we decided to find another home. And with great difficulty, we did just that.

The place we set our hearts upon was the vast unpopulated areas of America, fruitful and fit for habitation. There were no civil inhabitants there, but only brutish savages, little more than wild beasts, roaming up and down.

Fears About the New World

There were many opinions, fears, and doubts about the plan. Some encouraged it and others objected, trying to persuade everyone against it, saying the dangers were many and unimaginable. They argued that, aside from the perils of the sea, the journey was far too long for the weak bodies of women and the aged to endure. And if we survived crossing the ocean, there was still the desperate battle to survive in a harsh and unforgiving land. Lack of food and exposure to strange water and air would invite disease and bring the end of some of us or perhaps all.

Those who survived the perils of sea and land would still be in constant danger of cruel, merciless savages. They delight in bloody tortures, skinning their victims alive with clam shells. They cut off their arms and legs, piece by piece, roasting them and eating them before the very eyes of their barely living victims, and they inflicted other cruelties too horrible to mention. Stories like these couldn't help but bring down a paralyzing fear and trembling upon us, especially among the weak.

Some also argued that we could never raise enough money for the voyage, let alone the supplies. We learned of the failure of many such ocean crossings, and our frightening voyage to Holland years earlier was still fresh in our memories. Many said that it was already difficult enough to establish homes in Leiden with all the advantages of nearness, civility, and a wealthy society, none of which could be found in America.

All their objections were answered, however, by reminding them that every great and honorable deed is difficult and requires courage. Though the difficulties were many, they were not unbeatable. No one knew for certain whether we would face all these potential risks, and those we did face could be overcome with careful planning, patience, strength, and the help of God. Even in Holland we experienced poor conditions in a strange land.

No one should attempt these risks without good reason, but we were not merely seeking fortune or adventure. Because our motives were honorable and our quest was urgent, God may bless our risky endeavor. If we lost our lives in this undertaking, we would take comfort in the honor of our purpose.

Our misery could just grow worse of we remained in Leiden, for the truce between Spain and the Netherlands had ended. Nations were beating their drums and preparing for war. If the Spaniards invaded, they may be as cruel as any American savage. Famine and plague may spread just as rampant in Holland as in any place in America, and the liberty we enjoyed here may disappear.

There were endless arguments from both sides, but we finally reached an agreement. We would carry out our plan to settle in America as best we could.

QUESTIONS FOR REFLECTION AND DISCUSSION:

1. What were the main reasons the community wanted to leave Holland?

2. Compare the experience of their children to those in poorer nations today, and to your own children.

3. How can families and communities protect their values without completely isolating themselves from society?

4. Reflecting on the stories they heard about Native Americans, how can we avoid believing the worst about other cultures?

5. Bradford explains their departure from Leiden as honorable and worth the sacrifice. What accomplishments can you think of that came at great personal cost?

CHAPTER 5

Dreams of America

Our Difficult and Dangerous Decision
1617 - 1620

WE HUMBLY PRAYED for God's guidance and then discussed exactly where we should go. Some suggested Guiana on the coast of South America. Because of the warm climate there, we would not need heavy clothing or as many supplies. Guiana was an abundantly fruitful place where it is spring all year long. The plants there grew vigorously and effortlessly. And the Spaniards, who already controlled more regions than they could ever manage, were nowhere near Guiana.

Some rejected this plan, however, fearing that tropical regions harbored dreadful diseases that English bodies could not endure. And even if we prospered in Guiana, they said the Spanish would soon push us out and claim it for themselves, just as they did to the French in Florida.

We discussed the possibility of going to Virginia because Englishmen were already there. But if we lived under the authority of an authorized English colony, we might suffer the same religious persecution that we suffered in England. On the other hand, if we settled too far from other colonies we would also distance ourselves from any help and protection.

After all of our prayer, debate, and considerations, we finally reached a decision. We would live as a separate community under the oversight of the colony in Virginia, but request of King James to grant us religious freedom. We had prominent and influential friends who believed this could all be arranged, so we sent Robert Cushman and John Carver to England to make our formal request.

The Virginia Company of London was eager for us to join their American colony, assisting us in any way they could, however they were not able to guarantee our religious liberty. Many good and prominent men of the company tried to persuade the king and Archbishop Abbot to allow us religious freedom in America, but it was useless. The king gave assurance that he would not interfere with us if we remained peaceful, but he could not allow us religious freedom. Mr. Cushman and Mr. Carver then returned to Leiden to bring us their findings and the results of their negotiations.

Under the circumstances, many believed it was too risky to sell their homes and property for an American voyage. Some said it would have been better if we had not asked the king for such privileges, then to have asked and be rejected. But some leaders disagreed, saying that

King James (1566 – 1625) commissioned his new translation of the Bible in large part to help unite the various factions within the English church. The Pilgrims, however, continued their use of the Geneva Bible, which included doctrinal notes to which the king had objected.

we should proceed with our plans, for it was enough that the king promised not to interfere. The king did not make this promise official, however, but even an official promise would be worthless if the king later changed his mind. We concluded, therefore, it was best to rely on God's provision and not a king's promise.

After the decision, we sent Mr. Cushman and Mr. Carver back to London to negotiate with the Virginia Company for the best possible terms to use the land there, and to contact merchants and friends who were interested in our voyage. We told them clearly what conditions we would accept, and if they could not secure an agreement then they must wait for further instructions.

Securing the Help of Others

Below is a letter from Sir Edwin Sandys of the Virginia Company to our leaders in Leiden, Pastor Robinson and Elder Brewster:

> *London, England*
> *November 12, 1617*
>
> *After being warmly welcomed here, your representatives, Robert Cushman and John Carver, have communicated with the officials of his Majesty's Council for Virginia. We officially accept the seven articles you have written and signed and we have decided to go forward with your request, for both your benefit and that of the public.*
> *There are further details Mr. Cushman and Mr. Carver will share with you in person. Since they came*

here as responsible negotiators, representing many people, they requested more time to discuss the details of these plans with all those involved, and we willingly complied, so now they return to you.

If it pleases God to honor your plans, and you have no other hindrances, I trust you will understand that all our actions to assist you are the best that can reasonably be expected. And so I leave you with this plan (which I do hope is truly God's work) with the gracious protection and blessing of the Highest.

*Your very loving friend,
Edwin Sandys*

Pastor Robinson and Elder Brewster answered them as follows:

*Leiden, Holland
December 15, 1617*

Right Honorable One:

Acknowledging our debt, we are grateful for your remarkable love, especially in considering our needs for the weighty plans regarding Virginia. If repaying you becomes difficult, we shall ask God's assistance so that we will not fail to repay all that we owe you, showing respect for the love you have given us.

We have listed our requests as quickly and carefully as possible, signed by a majority of our congregation as you desired. John Carver, one of our church deacons, and another one of our men, will deliver these requests to you and the others in the Virginia Council. We fully authorize them with the administration of this matter.

We will not trouble you further regarding our care, for you have shown yourselves to be so concerned about us that, aside from God, we rely upon you more than anyone else in the world for your love, wisdom, and the support of your authorization.

To reassure you, here are some of the reasons we have planned this journey:

1. We truly believe the Lord is with us, and that he will graciously bless our endeavors according to the devotion of our hearts.
2. We are fully ready to leave the gentle care of our mother country and we are prepared for the difficulties of a strange and hard land.
3. The people in this venture are as hardworking and frugal as any people in the world.
4. We are knit together as one body in a strict and sacred covenant of the Lord. We shall not violate this bond which ties us together in looking after the welfare of each other and the community.
5. Unlike others before us, we will not be easily discouraged over trivial problems and seek to return home. Knowing how we were treated in both England and Holland, we know it would be even worse if we returned from America, for we would certainly receive no more comfort or help than we ever had before in our lives, which are now drawing short.

You may share this letter with the rest of the Virginia Council. We are grateful for their love and godliness toward us, as undeserving as we are. We will soon *leave and trouble you no more. We trust that Almighty God shall guide and direct you all. We are ever mindful that we are in your debt as well as any other supporters in the council.*

Obliged to you in all duty,
John Robinson and William Brewster

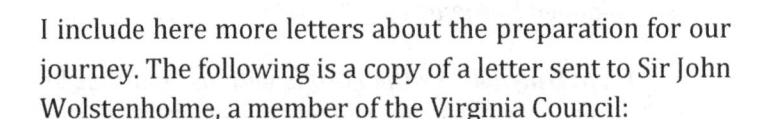

I include here more letters about the preparation for our journey. The following is a copy of a letter sent to Sir John Wolstenholme, a member of the Virginia Council:

Leiden, Holland,
January 27, 1618

Right Honorable One:

We are thankful for your remarkable help in our Virginia project, and we are aware of our indebtedness to you.

Enclosed you will find further explanation of our thoughts concerning the three points specified by his majesty's Honorable Private Council.

Though we are distressed by the unjust accusations made against us, we are grateful for the opportunity to clear ourselves before such honorable individuals.

We have enclosed both a brief explanation of our religious practices (which we believe is most suitable) and also a longer, more detailed one. You might prefer to show the longer document to the authorities instead of the first one.

Our prayer is that you may see the fruit of your good works continue through us. In this we shall not fail. Please let us know as soon as possible the result of your consultation with his majesty's Private Council, and any other directions you may have for us.

Reverently yours in all duty,
John Robinson and William Brewster

This is the brief explanation they mentioned:

Regarding the issues of church ministry, such as pastors who teach, elders who govern, and deacons who distribute the church's charitable contributions, as well as the two church sacraments of baptism and the Lord's supper, we completely agree in all points with the French Reformed Church as laid out in their confession of faith. We much prefer to take the Oath of Allegiance, pledging to be obedient English subjects. However, if that is not sufficient to you, we are willing to take the Oath of Supremacy, acknowledging the King as the head of the Church of England.

John Robinson and William Brewster

This is the longer, detailed explanation of our church:

Concerning the ministry of the church, as we formerly stated, we thoroughly agree with the public confession of faith of the French Reformed Church. There are, however, some small, incidental differences in our practices:

1. Our ministers pray with their heads uncovered. Ministers of the French church cover their heads.

2. We require that our church's governing elders be able to teach. The French church does not.

3. Our elders and deacons are chosen to serve indefinitely. Their elders and deacons are appointed for terms of one to three years.

4. In the case of public scandals, our elders administer reprimands and excommunications publicly before the church. Their elders, however, do so more privately in their church council.

5. We will only baptize an infant if at least one parent is a church member. Though this is different than some of their congregations, our practice does agree with the official public confession of the French Reformed Church and their church scholars.

We know of no other differences worth mentioning. Regarding taking an oath, please see the shorter declaration.

Signed,
John Robinson and William Brewster

The following is from Mr. Staresmore who delivered the above letters:

London, England
February 14, 1618

To Mr. Robinson:

I delivered your letter into the very hands of Sir John Wolstenholme as soon as I received it, and I remained there as he read it. There were two other papers enclosed with it. He read those and asked, "Who will appoint the church ministers for the new colony?"

I told him that the local church had the authority to do this, and that the most qualified church members ordained their minster by laying their hands upon him. I also told him that Christian ministers are either appointed by the pope or by the members of the church—and the pope is the Antichrist.

"Ho!" said Sir John. "We should all agree with the pope regarding issues like the doctrine of the Trinity, but let us not debate the papacy right now."

He also said that he would not show your letters to anyone for fear it may ruin your plans. He expected the Archbishop to appoint you as one of the ministers, but it seems you have disagreed with that plan.

I wish I knew the contents of your other two enclosures because he gave them much attention, especially the longer one.

I asked Sir John, "What good news do you have for me to write tomorrow?" and he indeed had very good news: both the king and the bishops have consented! Sir John said he would go to Chancellor Fulke Greville this very day and that he will tell me more next week.

Wednesday night I met with Sir Edwin Sandys who told me to be at the meeting of the Virginia Company of England next Wednesday, which I plan to do. I hope to have something certain for you next week.

I entrust you to the Lord.

Yours,
Sabine Staresmore

The negotiation process was long and difficult, with messengers going back and forth between England and Holland. On one occasion our messengers arrived in England only to find the Virginia Council so consumed in arguments that they couldn't accomplish a thing, which is clearly seen in this letter from our messenger:

London, England
May 8, 1619

Robert Cushman, to my loving friends in Leiden:

I wanted to write you for a long time, but could not until now. Even so, I still do not have the information I would like to give you. Though Mr. Brewster has probably written to Mr. Robinson, I thought it best for me to write to you also.

The main hindrance to our plans is the disagreement within the Virginia Company itself. They cannot get anything accomplished. Sir Thomas Smith complained to the company that he had too many duties as both Treasurer and Governor and he wished to be relieved. Then the company chose Sir Edwin Sandys to replace Smith as Treasurer and Governor. Mr. Sandys had sixty votes, Sir John Wolstenholme had sixteen, and Alderman Johnson had twenty-four.

Sir Thomas was somehow insulted by the vote, becoming angry and prodding some to challenge the election. He then attempted to disgrace Sir Edwin, forcing him out as Governor. The company remains stuck in controversy and cannot do any business. We still don't know what will happen. Sir Edwin will probably prevail, and if he does, things will go well with our Virginia plans. If not, things will get worse. We hope the courts will resolve the matter in two or three days.

Meanwhile, I plan to go to Kent for two or three weeks, unless the controversy continues or we receive bad news about our Virginia plans.

Captain Samuel Argall returned home this week from the Virginia settlement in America. When he received notice in Virginia that the council wanted to replace him as the deputy Governor there, he left before his replacement (Sir George Yeardley) arrived, which created even more controversy. He was a welcome presence here, but he brought heartbreaking news about the ship called the William and Thomas, which carried Elder Francis Blackwell and his people.

They sailed too far south due to the northwest winter winds. The shipmaster and six crewmen were dying, and it was a terribly long search for the Chesapeake Bay. The ship full of settlers didn't arrive in Virginia until March—six months after leaving England. Mr. Blackwell and Captain Maggner are both dead.

Mr. Argall has informed us that, of the 180 people that were tightly packed on that ship, 130 of them are now dead. They lacked fresh water and were afflicted with diarrhea. Some people here in London were actually surprised, not at the number of the dead, but at how many of them were actually still alive. The merchants blame Mr. Blackwell for packing them in like fish onto that small ship.

When the group was preparing for the voyage, many grumbled and complained, pointing the blame at

Mr. Blackwell for the pitiful, thoughtless conditions of the journey. The streets of Gravesend, from which they set sail, were filled with heated quarrels at the time. Passengers cried out, "It this what you've brought me to? Should I thank you for this?"

It is difficult news to hear, and I wonder if it may change our plans. No one here wants to halt our endeavor, however, but instead learn from those tragedies and make any suitable adjustments.

As we attempt to "serve one another in love" (Gal. 5:13), let us not become enchanted by overbearing people, especially those like Mr. Blackwell who seek their own interests. It worries me that we are all inexperienced learners in this project and none of us are teachers. However it is better than learning from a teacher like Mr. Blackwell. His idea to take along Pastor Francis Johnson's congregation to Virginia was their tragic undoing. Mr. Blackwell may have escaped the king's punishment for his earlier dishonesty, but now he has been finally and fatally caught.

Captain Argall's ship has yet to arrive at our port, so we have no letters from the Virginia settlement yet, just the Captain's personal reports, and it appears he left Virginia in secrecy. The William *and* Thomas, *which carried Mr. Blackwell and his party, will soon return. Pastor Robinson was right when he once said that we would not hear anything good about those people.*

Mr. Brewster is not well. I don't know if he will return to you or go north. I plan to stay here until I finish our business, though I am sorry to be away so long. If things had gone more quickly, I could have returned within two weeks.

I pray that God will direct us and give us a suitable spirit for our business.

In this letter I have summarized the issues that Mr. Brewster has written about more extensively to Mr. Robinson.
I now leave you to the Lord's protection.

Yours in all readiness,
Robert Cushman

The Immorality of Mr. Blackwell

A few words about Mr. Francis Blackwell. He was a well-known church elder in Amsterdam. Both he and Pastor Johnson turned away from the truth of the Scriptures by granting their church elders far too much authority. Tragically, they pulled many Christians away to create their own faction, dishonoring God, scandalizing the truth, and tarnishing their reputations.

He and other godly people were preparing a secret voyage to Virginia, but their plans were discovered. They were caught in a secret meeting in London. Many were arrested, including Mr. Blackwell, but he flattered the bishops and twisted and denied his true Christian beliefs about church authority in order to comply with the Church of England. In a more devious move to avoid arrest he betrayed Mr. Sabin Staresmore to church authorities, a godly man who escaped the meeting undetected.

They dismissed Mr. Blackwell's case, and the archbishop authorized him to take his followers to Virginia. Though he won the favor of the bishop, he lost the favor of the Lord. If a fate such as Mr. Blackwell's comes from the bishop's approval, happy are they that do not receive it. It was a final and fatal voyage for him and nearly all his people. In either life or death, it's better to keep both a good conscience and the Lord's approval.

Both he and his followers are likely buried beneath the sea; even so I pray the Lord will be merciful and bring their souls to rest in that Haven of Happiness.

Here is a letter from Mr. Staresmore, the man that Mr. Blackwell betrayed to authorities:

From my cell in Wood Street Prison
London, England
September 4, 1618

To my dear friend and Christian brother, John Carver:

I greet you and yours in the Lord.
Brother Richard Masterson has told you about my situation. He also would have been arrested along with me if he and his home were as well-known as mine. I have also written to Robert Cushman to explain to him how I am doing.
Twice I have petitioned the Sheriff, and once to Sir Edward Coke, trying to win their sympathy. If they weren't overruled by others, I would probably be free soon. I am only a young man and I am out of money, living on credit. Now financially obligated to people in this city, I have overwhelming debt and I am stuck in a dreary and cramped prison. Besides paying heavy rent abroad, my business is at a standstill. My only servant is helplessly waiting for me, and my wife is about to give birth, but I can do nothing until the Lords of His Majesty's Council give consent.
Francis Blackwell, however, who is just as involved

in these plans as I am, was easily freed. Not only did he receive less punishment, but he received the Archbishop's blessing. My heart is broken by Mr. Blackwell's immorality and I hope it gets no worse. He and others, however, are not brokenhearted over my misery. They even claim that betraying me to the authorities was a good thing because my arrest helped gain their freedom to settle in Virginia. Since the authorities found out about our secret meeting, Mr. Blackwell says he could only gain his freedom by turning in someone else.

I expect to know my fate soon. Later I'll write to others in your church. They can tell you what happens.

I've nothing else to say, so I entrust myself to your prayers, placing us all in the hands of the Lord.

Your friend and brother in bonds,
Sabin Staresmore

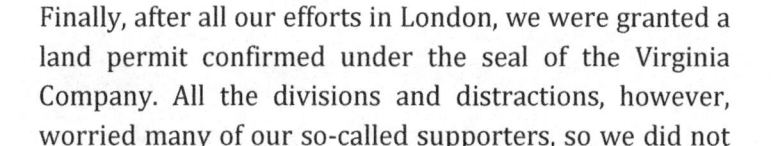

Finally, after all our efforts in London, we were granted a land permit confirmed under the seal of the Virginia Company. All the divisions and distractions, however, worried many of our so-called supporters, so we did not receive all the financing we had hoped for.

Some friends advised us to have the permit written in the name of Mr. John Wincop instead of someone in our own group. Mr. Wincop was a religious gentleman who worked for the Countess of Lincoln and he planned to sail with us. Evidently it was not God's will for him to join us, so we never used that permit which cost us so much in time and money to acquire.

The permit was sent to us in Leiden for review, along

with the terms regarding the merchants and friends that might sail with us. Along with those papers came further conditions from Mr. Thomas Weston and his associates who were financing the voyage and settlement, and they asked us to quickly prepare for the journey.

All that business about the land permit just symbolizes the uncertainty of the things in this world; even after we toil over them, they still vanish into smoke.

QUESTIONS FOR REFLECTION AND DISCUSSION:

1. What were the pros and cons for the Separatists to live in the territory of Virginia?

2. How did the King of England and the Archbishop complicate their plans?

3. In their letter to Sir Edwin Sandys and the Virginia Company, Pastor Robinson and William Brewster gave several reasons for their voyage to America. Which reasons seem most compelling to you and why? Which of their claims would you doubt most and why?

4. One objection that the Separatists had to the Catholic Church and the Church of England was that they did not allow their people to choose their own leaders. How might this issue be relevant in America and Western nations today?

5. Explain their difficulties in getting the Virginia Council to approve their venture.

6. Robert Cushman writes about another ship of religious refugees who sailed to America. Describe the experience of Francis Blackwell and his people. How might that news have impacted Bradford's community? How might such a story impact you if you were one of the Pilgrims?

CHAPTER 6

Negotiations

Our Dealings with Greed and Grievance
1620

WE FINALLY RECEIVED the documents outlining the arrangements and our entire church in Leiden held a solemn meeting, a day of humble worship to seek the Lord's direction. Pastor Robinson gave us a message from 1Samuel 23:3-4: "And David's men said to him, 'See, we are afraid here in Judah. How much more, then, if we come to Keilah against the Philistine armies?' Then David inquired of the Lord yet again."

He shared many lessons about our situation from this text, strengthening us against fear and confusion, encouraging our resolve. After his message, we decided who and how many should prepare to leave first. Not all who were willing to emigrate could get their affairs in order so quickly. Even if they could, we did not have the means to send everyone at once.

Most people in our church could not yet leave, so for that reason and others Pastor Robinson decided to remain in Holland for now. For spiritual guidance, William Brewster, one of our church elders, would make the journey with us.

We all agreed that those of us who sailed to America would become a separate congregation outside the authority of the Leiden church. The voyage would be long and dangerous, and we could not be certain that we would ever meet again in this world. However, if any people from one congregation crossed the ocean to join the other, we agreed to readily welcome them as members of that local church. If the Lord allowed them life, means, and opportunity, those who remained in Leiden promised they would join us as soon as possible.

While we considered all the purchases and hiring that our voyage required, and the confusing proceedings of the Virginia Company, some Dutchmen approached us with a fair offer to sail with them. It was then, however, that we first met Mr. Thomas Weston.

Mr. Weston was a London merchant, and well-acquainted with some people in our church. He came to us in Leiden with an enticing offer. After meeting with our pastor and other leaders, he persuaded us not to deal with the Dutch, nor depend too much on the Virginia Company. He said that we should prepare for our journey without worrying about money or supplies, for he and his partners had now come to our aid, and he promised we would have everything we needed.

Our task now, Mr. Weston told us, was simply to

draw up articles of agreement that would encourage his friends to invest in our venture. He carefully reviewed our written proposals, and after his approval we sent them to England with two of our men, John Carver and Robert Cushman. There they would deliver the docu-

William Bradford (c. 1590 - 1657) was chosen governor of Plymouth after John Carver's death in 1620. He served several various terms until 1656.

ments, receive the promised funds, and make all the necessary arrangements for our voyage strictly according to our written agreements. Those in Leiden who planned to sail with us were told to prepare their estates, sell their property, and gather funds for the voyage. We all contributed our money to a common fund, and appointees would later distribute the resources to us as needed to purchase our supplies.

We learned from Mr. Weston and others that some English noblemen received a large land grant from the king for the northern parts of America. The area was part of the Virginia Company's permit, however it would not be under their authority. The northern region would be called "New England." Because of the profitable fishing there, among other reasons, Mr. Weston and our church leaders decided that this was the best place to settle.

The Work of Reaching Agreements

As in all business, the actual doing is more difficult than the planning, especially trying to get everyone to agree. Some people in England who had agreed to the journey had now changed their minds. Some of our investors backed out, making several excuses. Among the potential voyagers, some were upset that we were not going to Guiana. Others said they would only go to Virginia, while still others said they would settle anywhere but Virginia. There was so much confusion that those of us who had already sold our property in Leiden, and contributed our money to the general fund, became afraid of what might happen. In the end, the majority finally decided we would settle in New England.

More difficulty arose when Mr. Weston and his partners demanded that the agreements we all made in Leiden must be altered. These changes, he claimed, would attract more investors to the project. If we did not receive full financial support, then all our plans would be ruined, and many of us had already sold our property and placed our money in the general fund. In view of the dire circumstances, the two representatives we sent to England agreed to the newly revised terms—which was contrary to our earlier instructions. Mr. Carver and Mr. Cushman later told us that they had not consulted those of us in Leiden about the revised terms because it would just further delay the voyage. Needless to say, when we learned of it all, there was much contention. Here are the new terms that Mr. Weston demanded:

July 1, 1620

The Merchant Adventurers Company and settlers all agree:

1. That for everyone sixteen years old or older who joins this venture, their participation shall be considered as equal to a financial investment of ten English pounds, and they shall be awarded a single share of stock in the project.

2. That a person who also furnishes ten pounds in either money or supplies shall be regarded as investing a total of twenty English pounds, and shall receive a double share of the stock.

3. That both settlers and the Merchant Adventurers Company shall continue their joint stock ownership and partnership for seven years, unless the entire partnership agrees to discontinue due to unforeseen circumstances. During this time all profits and benefits received by any means whatsoever shall remain in the common stock until it is divided between them.

4. That upon their arrival the settlers shall assign several fit men to the ships and boats for the task of fishing while the others build houses, till the soil, plant crops, and produce goods useful for the colony.

5. That at the end of the seven years all profits and property shall be equally divided between the Merchant Adventurers Company and the settlers. When this is done, everyone shall be free from any and all obligations to the other partners of this venture.

6. That whoever may join the colony after this, or puts anything into the stock, shall at the end of the seven years be paid in proportion to his time at the colony.

7. That he who brings his wife and children or servants shall be allowed another share of stock for every person sixteen years old or older. A double share shall be allotted per person if the necessary provisions are made as stated in item number two. If the additional persons are between the ages of ten and sixteen, then two of them shall be considered as equal in monetary value to one person for purposes of transportation fees and division of investment and profits.

8. That children who are now under the age of ten will have no allotted share in the stock, but shall be assigned fifty acres of unworked land.

9. That the share of those who die before the end of the seven year commitment shall be transferred to new share owners according to the length of their time within the colony.

10. That all settlers are to have their food, drink, clothing, and all provisions supplied by the common stock and supplies of the colony.

There are two main grievances we had with these new terms. First, we believed the houses, improved lands, and our gardens should all be owned by the settlers alone at the end of the seven year commitment instead of a joint ownership between settlers and merchants. Second, we settlers should be allowed two days off each week to work on private projects for ourselves and our families, however the new terms did not specify this.

Because letters are the best record of history, in the following you will learn more about our grievances from our own letters so you may better understand.

Here is a letter from Pastor John Robinson to our representative, John Carver:

Leiden, Holland
June 24, 1620

My dear friend and brother:

I always remember you and your family with great affection, and never cease praying earnestly to God for your welfare.

From our letters, you thoroughly understand our pitiful situation here. We are in desperate need of a ship and we do not see any likely means of getting one. There is also a great lack of money for our needed supplies.

As you know, Edward Pickering will not even provide a penny here, and Robert Cushman was counting on him and others for hundreds of pounds. It seems strange that we were referred to him and his partners for a financial investment, though Mr. Weston writes that he received one hundred more pounds from him. These negotiations seem mysterious, as does the whole affair.

Some people say they'll contribute part of their own money, but not until our transportation is secured, or at least until they see plans to acquire it. I don't think there is even one man here who would actually pay anything, even if he now had the money in his own wallet.

You recall that we all chose to depend solely on Mr. Weston and whatever resources he could secure. When the Dutchmen offered us a deal, we refused it based upon Mr. Weston's insistence and the conditions he offered us. I believe he was sincerely concerned about our situation, but so far he is not following through. Many think that by now he should have already given us our promised funds. As a merchant, however, I know he can presently use those funds, whereas if he had already handed it over to us, we may have spent it all by now.

But I cannot ignore the fact that he has still not yet arranged shipping for us, nor has he told us how he intends to acquire it. Someone told me that when Mr. Weston is prodded about the issue of the ship, he avoids the subject and refers people to someone else. He would also ask the merchant George Morton for the latest information as if he himself had little to do with the project.

We don't know if the delay is because some of Mr. Weston's financial partners are not coming through, or if he is afraid that, after everyone is ready to leave, he'll find that shipping costs are greater than he estimated. Maybe he thinks that withholding funds from us will put us in a bind, and will therefore encourage Thomas Brewer and Mr. Pickering to invest even more. We *don't know what is going on, but we do know that things are not falling into place as we need them.*

Mr. Weston seems quite happy about our plans to hire a ship, but we have done nothing about it for at least two reasons: first of all, we are depending upon Robert Cushman, and while he is a good and talented man, he is not a negotiator. He seems indifferent to our specified terms and has done nothing but offer additional terms and suggestions. Secondly, while we have general plans, we are still lacking in details and the means to accomplish such a daunting project.

Mr. Weston says that he also has plans to hire out a ship. I wish he would do it, but I have little hope. You know what to expect of Thomas Brewer, but I do not think Mr. Pickering will participate outside of helping us buy the use of a ship (as said in previous letters).

About the conditions—you know what we think of the agreements. Keep this foremost in mind: with the current terms, most of the colony will likely be consumed with fishing and trading instead of working the land and building homes. The land and houses are not nearly as crucial to investors, but the most current agreement, which divides the property between the colony and the investors, will discourage settlers who would otherwise work hard day and night, building good, comfortable homes for themselves.

This constant work of the majority is a good reason to allow them two days off each week (as we first agreed) for personal needs. Imagine how it would be if you would work seven straight years for someone else without one day off.

Let me know who will be going, how many, what skills they have, and any other details. I wish you could have remained in London for all these negotiations, however I know you were busy gathering provisions.

Time is running short, so I must bid you and yours farewell. Always in the Lord, in whom I rest.

At your service,
John Robinson.

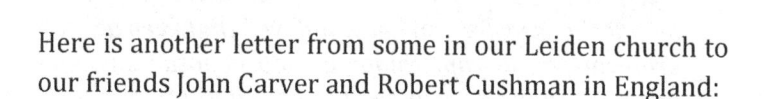

Here is another letter from some in our Leiden church to our friends John Carver and Robert Cushman in England:

Leiden, Holland
June 10, 1620

Good Brothers:

Mr. Thomas Nash delivered some very encouraging letters to us. Many here were about ready to give up on this voyage until you sent him our way. Part of the problem is the new terms that you arranged. Everyone is against them! Another problem is our inability to accomplish any of the important tasks you request.

You, Mr. Cushman, asked us what we do not like about the new conditions. You say that you are even willing to change them just so we will not consider you brainless. We have referred you to the former recommendations from our pastors, and we just want you to follow them.

Please do not obligate us to unreasonable demands, such as giving up half of our homes and land to the investors after we finally fulfill a seven year commitment! Nor do we approve of losing our two days off from work each week, as we had previously agreed. We need that time to attend to our personal affairs. What is the use of bringing servants with us to attend to our needs if they are not even allowed time to do so?

Your messenger Mr. Nash had to tell us about these problems since you did not put them in your letters. We do hope that you have not changed any other terms without asking us. Please remember the pre-arranged conditions that we all agreed to and put down in writing. You are required to stay within those terms. We are all shocked, for you know full well that even a small problem can disrupt things during negotiations, and most of us don't even understand all this business.

Greet Mr. Weston for us. We hope he is being honest with us. Please let him know our situation. Show him our letters if you think it might help. Tell him we are counting on him, because if he had not planned to invest in our venture, we would never have agreed to it. We assume that if he did not have the means to fulfill his agreement, he would not have partnered with us in the first place. Therefore, we hope that he will follow through with his obligations. Since we've plainly explained our situation to you, we hope you will help us.

We seek God's help, who is able to pull us from these struggles by his care for his children. We desire to see his hand working for us in this venture that we all do in his name.

Your perplexed, yet hopeful brothers,
Samuel Fuller
Edward Winslow
William Bradford
Isaac Allerton

A letter to the Leiden church from Robert Cushman in London:

London, England

Brothers,

I understand from your letters and other messages that you are terribly unhappy with how I've handled the negotiations. I'm sorry to hear that, but I believe I can convince any reasonable person that I am handling this correctly. Some people tell me I should return to Leiden to explain my actions to you, but under the circumstances I cannot be gone even for a day without risking our planned voyage. I do not see what good it would do to return now anyway.

Let me put you at ease. Regarding the change in one item of the conditions, if you fully understood the situation you would not blame me. When John Carver first brought over the articles of agreement to London, Mr. Weston was the only one from the Merchant Adventurers Company who had seen it and approved of it.

Sir George Farrer and his brother withdrew five-hundred pounds from the project, and all the other potential investors (except Mr. Weston) would have withdrawn their funds if we did not change that one clause. It was not my fault that we had settled upon the conditions of the agreement while we were all in Leiden without even consulting those in London who would financially support our journey.

Also, I have already written to you about the fairness of that condition despite the inconveniences, which should answer the concerns raised by Pastor Robinson. Without altering that one clause, we would not receive the funds to get there, nor would we gain the very supplies we need to survive.

Yet, despite the important reasons for these changes (which were not my ideas in the first place), and without any good arguments against them, I hear all of these complaints against me. You claim that I'm taking things over and making conditions more fit for thieves and slaves than honest men.

Here are your arguments about the clause in question and my responses to them:

1. You argue that these terms favor the poor if we cannot divide the land and homes among those settlers who had invested their own money.

My answer: True. This shows the inequality of our circumstances. We should not show favoritism to those who can invest both labor and money over those who can only invest their labor.

2. Another answer regarding the poor: Remember, we are not giving charity, but building a storehouse together. For seven years, no one will be poorer than anyone else. In this arrangement, if anyone is rich then no one can be poor. There will be no reason for anyone to complain of poverty or beg for handouts. People request charity for calamities, not business ventures.

3. You say that prohibiting private ownership will keep people from building nice, beautiful houses, which is not good politics.

Answer: That is how it should be. We should build the kind of homes for now that we would not mind burning down if we ever needed to flee at night by the light of the flames. Our riches will not be in flamboy-

ance, but in our strength. If God sends us riches, we'll use them to provide more men, ships, ammunition, and other essentials. Good political thinking should tell you that a community will more likely shrink than grow if fine houses and fancy clothes become the issue.

4. *You suggest that the government should simply ban the construction of elaborate homes so that we could still allow private home ownership without the risk of excessively pretentious houses.*
Answer: If we decide beforehand that we will all have the same simple homes, then government involvement is unnecessary.

5. *You say not everyone has the same position in life.*
Answer: If by "position" you mean wealth, you are mistaken. There is more to wealth than money. If by "position" you mean quality, then I say that someone who is unhappy with his neighbor having an equally good house, food, or other things such as he has, he is not a good "quality" person. Those who are mainly concerned with their status in society are better off living in solitude than in any civil or religious community.

6. *You say that such simple homes have little value—hardly worth five English pounds.*
Answer: True. They may not even be worth half that. But if a simple home is adequate, then why worry about it? Why should we give anyone any reason to accuse us of being materialistic and greedy?

7. *You suggest that our current investors, the Merchant Adventurers Company, are not as interested in generating profit as the previous investors were.*
Answer: Then they are better for us than those who

might pull out of the project for the small issue of profit. Brothers, beware of having profit as your main goal. Either change your attitudes or stay home, otherwise you will end up like Jonah trying to flee to Tarshish (Jonah 1:3-15). Some are more concerned with profit than others. Ventures like these are made with all kinds of people and we must try to work with them all if possible.

8. You say that these new conditions "will break the structure of our community for many reasons we could give you."

Answer: So you say. But I say these new conditions will create a closer community "for many reasons that I could give you."

9. You're concerned our investors would likely become even wealthier by our labor in fishing and shipping.

Answer: If our venture is profitable for them, then it will be profitable for us. In addition to our right to live on the land, half of the profit will be ours. And if we can make much money from fishing and shipping, then there is even less of a need to work the land, and our homes and land would be therefore less important to us anyway.

10. You say that our risk is now greater than that of our investors with these new conditions.

Answer: True, but they are not forcing us into this venture. Wasn't this project our idea in the first place? If we decided not to go after all, then they would be very content to keep their money.

So, I have now offered some answers to help loosen the knots you have given me. I hope you will seriously con-

sider them and not give me any more difficulties about the negotiations.

I have heard your complaints about the "slave-like obligations" I have created, but I have honestly altered very little from the original conditions, and now I have explained the reasons for those revisions. If you are worried about having no more than two days a week for personal business, you worry needlessly. Take three days or a week for all I care. The investors simply want us to be reasonable men of integrity, able to be trusted with our labor.

Regarding the church in Amsterdam, I did not think that they would join our venture anyway. They despise our Christian freedom and we despise their harsh rigidity. If my actions discourage them from joining us, then let them back out. I will refund their investment immediately. Or if the congregation decides I should stay, then very well. I will be content with merely the clothes on my back. Now let us have some peace and no more haggling. I certainly did not expect all these problems.

Yours,
Robert Cushman

I don't recall whether those of us in Leiden ever received the above letter from Mr. Cushman. John Carver may have kept it so we would not become even angrier. But we did receive this following letter from him:

London, England
June 11, 1620

Greetings to you in Leiden:

Yesterday I received your letter through John Turner, and another from Amsterdam by way of Mr. W.

Between our problems here and your complaints there, I nearly handed the whole project over to John Carver. Thinking again, however, I decided to give it another try and let Mr. Weston know how shaky things are. He has not been happy with us lately. He said he would forget the whole business if he had not already promised us. But considering, among other things, how deep we already are in this project he said he will still follow through.

We decided to hire a ship. We found a small one, but the only other larger one we could get was too large for us. This small one is a fine ship, though. Since our dear friends there in Leiden are so particular, we hope to secure the ship without upsetting them any further. But if you consider the ship too small, perhaps that is for the best, then those who are not happy with the new agreement that I arranged will have a reason to wait until the seven year contract has passed. If you attended to this business a month ago and had written these things to us earlier, we all could have been done by now. So be it.

I hope our friends there will be all the more encouraged to venture with us, assuming you are pleased with the hiring of this ship. All I need you to do now is to purchase salt and nets. The rest I can acquire here. If you cannot buy it now, then have the shop owners give you credit for a month or two and we will pay them all later. Have Mr. Reynolds stay there and send his ship *the* Speedwell *to Southampton. We have hired another ship pilot here, Captain John Clark, who recently took a ship full of cattle to Virginia just last year.*

John Turner will be there Tuesday night, I believe, and he will tell you more. I had considered returning with him to address the accusations many of you have made against me, but I'm more concerned about finishing this business than arguing. I am just too busy to deal with complaints.

I do hope my true friends will not doubt that I have reasons for my actions. If there is any confusion regarding water or other issues, I will explain later. For now, please ask our friends to not judge me so quickly. If I make mistakes in these affairs, remember it was you who sent me, so blame yourselves and then send someone else so I can go back to my job of cleaning wool.

I am willing to have my actions judged by both God and men, so when we meet again I will explain all the work I've done here. The Lord, who rightly judges without respect to persons (1Pet. 1:17), sees how fair I am. May he grant us peaceful and patient minds in all of this turmoil.

And now I leave you in all love and affection.
I hope we will all be ready here in fourteen days.

Your humble brother,
Robert Cushman

Contrary to what Mr. Weston and Mr. Cushman recommended, most of the supplies were acquired at Southampton and then differences later arose among those in

England who were preparing them. More people from London, Billericay, and elsewhere decided to join us on the voyage, so those of us in Holland thought it best that these strangers choose someone they trust to help Mr. Carver and Mr. Cushman make preparations. This would help prevent any appearance of favoritism as they gathered supplies. The strangers chose Christopher Martin from Billericay. This complicated the process, but it also showed them our fairness and honesty. Some of these issues are addressed in this letter from Mr. Cushman to Mr. Carver:

London, England
June 10, 1620

Robert Cushman to John Carver in Leiden:

Loving friend,

I just received letters from you, filled with both affection and complaints. I don't know what you want from me. You accuse me of negligence, which makes me wonder why you chose such a negligent man like me in the first place. You know that I will do everything in my power to keep from being behind even one hour. I guarantee it!

You claim that Mr. Weston will help us with money above and beyond his promised share, yet he complains to me that if he had not already agreed to help us he would have done nothing more. He believes we are reckless and he is upset that our supplies are being gathered so far away and that he was also not informed of how much we really needed. He also believes that since the preparations are being made in three different locations, all remote from one another, we are making things unnecessarily difficult and we will not be able to leave until after summer.

Let's be honest: there is already division among us! We are more prepared for an argument than a voyage. Since you left I have received three letters from you there in Leiden, but since they are all about me I will not bother you by discussing them now. I have always feared that those in Amsterdam would want to join us. You must choose to either leave them behind or me. Otherwise there will be quarreling.

Aside from the crewmen, we have calculated one hundred fifty people for this voyage. Including all the funds you've acquired, we cannot come up with more than about 1200 pounds, not counting a few items such as cloth, stockings, and shoes. So we are now short at least three or four hundred pounds. I would have preferred less beer and other supplies in favor of something else. We could get that in Amsterdam or Kent, but now it will be hard to get it there without more unwanted pressure.

You're afraid that we've begun building something we can't finish (Luke 14:28-30). Indeed, we made our plans without adequate consultation, so perhaps we have reason to fear. There was disagreement among the three of us from the very beginning. You wrote to Mr. Martin, telling him not to make provisions in Kent (which he did anyway), and you spelled out to him how much he should get of everything—without considering anyone else's input or objections. One who refuses to listen to others acts more like a king than a partner.

If things do not change, our partnership will display argument and accusation instead of humility and peace. However, we will soon provide you with the money you need there. You say five hundred pounds will be enough. The rest, which we'll need both here and in Holland, we will scrape up somehow. You write that Pastor Crabe has promised to go with us. I hope so. But because of his former opposition, I won't believe it until I see it.

Think the best of everyone, and be patient with what is still lacking.

May the Lord guide us all.

Your loving friend,
Robert Cushman

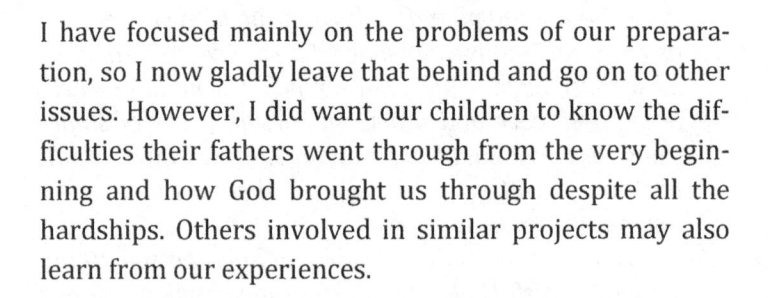

I have focused mainly on the problems of our preparation, so I now gladly leave that behind and go on to other issues. However, I did want our children to know the difficulties their fathers went through from the very beginning and how God brought us through despite all the hardships. Others involved in similar projects may also learn from our experiences.

QUESTIONS FOR REFLECTION AND DISCUSSION:

1. Thomas Weston went to Holland and promised to solve all their problems in moving to America. Should they have been suspicious of him? Explain. Has anyone promised you easy solutions to complicated problems?

2. After many of the Separatists in Holland sold their homes and invested into a common account, the Merchant Adventurers Company of London insisted on changing the terms for financing their settlement. What would you do if you were one of the Separatists?

3. What are some of the greatest concerns those in Leiden had with Mr. Weston and his partners?

4. Why were those in Holland so upset with their representatives in London (Robert Cushman and John Carver)?

5. How did Mr. Cushman defend himself against the criticisms of his friends?

6. What do you think of Mr. Cushman's opinions about wealth, poverty, and community?

7. Cushman became exasperated, caught between the demands of his friends in Holland on the one hand and the demands of Weston and his partners on the other. What would you do in his situation?

CHAPTER 7

Saying Goodbye

Hearts Break as We Sail
July - August 1620

AFTER ALL THE TRAVELING and purchases, we were finally ready for the voyage. We bought the services of a small sixty ton ship called the *Speedwell* and prepared it in Holland. The ship and her crew would remain with us for one year in the New Land for fishing and other needs. The *Mayflower*, a one hundred eighty ton ship, was hired in London. Everything else was made ready for the journey.

After all was prepared, we held a day of worship to humble ourselves before the Lord. Our pastor used Ezra 8:21 as his text: "I proclaimed a fast at the river of Ahava, that we might humble ourselves before our God, to seek from him a safe journey for us, and for our children and all our possessions."

His words were well chosen for the occasion. The rest

of the time was spent in earnest prayer and much tears.

When it came time to leave, most of the church accompanied us out of the city to Delfshaven, a town some thirty miles away, where the ship awaited. So we left Leiden, the good and pleasant city that was our home for nearly twelve years. But we knew that we were pilgrims[12] and we were not swayed by our challenges, for we looked to heaven which was our dearest country, and so our spirits were calmed.

When we arrived, the ship and everything was ready. Many friends, even some from Amsterdam, came to see us off. Most of them had little sleep that night, but we had warm conversations with friends, we spoke of our Christian faith, and shared our Christian love for each other.

The wind was good the next day, so we boarded the ship as our friends watched. This was in late July, 1620. Everyone was crying. Important words were shared that pierced the heart. Even some of the Dutch people watching nearby could not keep from crying. It was wonderful to see such expressions of love. It was difficult to leave, but the tide was right and it would not wait for anyone. We all kneeled in prayer with our pastor as he tearfully asked for God's blessing upon us. With tears and embraces we said our goodbyes. It proved to be the very last time many of us would ever see each other.

Because of the good wind, we soon arrived at Southampton on the Southern coast of England. The *Mayflower* and her crew were waiting there along with the other

---

[12] Hebrews 11:13.

voyagers. After warm greetings we got down to the final details of the business, wanting to be quickly done with it all and discuss the changes in our agreement.

Mr. Carver claimed he was occupied in Southampton, and was unaware of the negotiations going on in London. Mr. Cushman claimed he only did what was necessary and fair, or else all our plans would fall through. He said he informed his partners from the beginning about what he was doing, and they agreed and let him carry on. He received the money in London and sent it to those in Southampton to purchase the supplies, though he and some of the Merchant Adventurers preferred to prepare them someplace else. When we asked why he did not consult us about altering the terms, Mr. Cushman said there was not enough time. Debating the changes would slow down the whole project, he said, and it was already so late in the year that it was too risky to wait any longer. We were not satisfied with his explanations.

Voicing Complaints to the Investors

Mr. Weston came from London to see us off, and to confirm the new conditions with us, but we refused, telling him that he knew very well how different they were from our original agreement. Besides, Mr. Carver and Mr. Cushman did not have the authority to make any agreements without the consent of those of us in Leiden. In fact, we specifically told them not to agree to any new conditions. Mr. Weston became angry, and informed us that we would receive no more assistance from him.

This was the first point of contention between us and Mr. Weston. And though we still needed more money for the voyage (nearly one hundred pounds), he would not give us a penny more, so we were forced to sell some of our provisions for the extra funds. We had an excess of butter, so we sold thirty to forty casks of it.

As we waited in Southampton, we wrote a letter to the Merchant Adventurers Company about the changes in our agreement:

Southampton
August 3, 1620

Beloved friends,

We are sorry as we write this because, first of all, we expected to see most of you here, but we are especially sorry because of our disagreements. Since we cannot meet with you personally, we think we should write down our legitimate complaints regarding the terms negotiated between you and Robert Cushman without our knowledge or approval. He says that it was all for good reason, but that does not justify it.

Our primary complaint is in the fifth and ninth articles regarding the division of houses and land. As you know, one of the main motivations for our voyage was the prospect of owning our own homes and acreage. In fact this was considered so reasonable that when your representative Mr. Weston explained the conditions to us, he himself wrote that one down. A copy of it was sent to you with some additions of our own. It was approved by both us and your company. A payment date was set, and those of us in Holland have indeed paid.

After that, Robert Cushman, John Peirce, and Christopher Martin put the revised articles down in better form, and recorded them in a book. When Mr. Cushman delivered a copy to William Mullins, he then put in his investment.

Aside from someone's personal copy, we in Holland had never seen an official agreement until we arrived here in Southampton. And when we saw the changes in the conditions we voiced complete disapproval. But we have already sold our estates and are ready to travel, so it is too late for us to back out. We beg you to consider these issues objectively. If a mistake has been made, put the blame where it belongs and not on us. We have far more justification to support the original agreement than you have for supporting the second.

We never authorized Mr. Cushman to draw up even one article for us. We only sent him to receive the funds for the agreements we had already made and to gather supplies and assist John Carver when he arrived. However, since you consider yourselves just as wronged as we do, we have amended the ninth article in a way that we believe will solve the problem.

We are not selfish people who only care about our own wishes. Therefore, to show our friends and financial supporters that we also value your concerns, we have added one last article to the agreement. We hereby promise that if we do not gain large profits within the seven years, then if the Lord allows we will continue our partnership with you. We hope this will satisfy you since we are now convinced that the other arrangements will not work.

We're in such desperate need that we had to sell some provisions just to acquire another sixty pounds of funds to sail out of the harbor. Now we hardly have any butter, oil, or extra soles to mend our shoes. Nor do we have enough swords, muskets, or armor for our men. However, we are willing to trust God and take all these risks so no one will speak evil of God because of us.

We now salute you all in love, asking the Lord to bless our endeavors and keep our hearts in the bonds of peace and love.

We shall take our leave and close.

Yours,

Pastor Robinson's Heart

The letter above was signed by many of our leaders. The following letter was written by Pastor Robinson to John Carver, and it was the last letter Mr. Carver lived to receive from him. You can see here the tender love and care of a true pastor:

July 27, 1620

My dear Brother,

With your last letter was the note of information which I will carefully keep and use when there is occasion. I sense your bewilderment and exhaustion. You have always comforted others in their trials, so I hope you will care for yourself so that if greater difficulties press upon you, you will not be crushed, as the Apostle Paul has said (2Cor. 4:8). I know your spirit will sustain you.

Things will be better when you enjoy the presence

and help of so many godly brothers. They will help carry your load. Whatever they think of others, they will not suspect you of negligence or presumption.

What else can I say to you and your good wife other than I love you in the Lord as much as my own soul, and I always will. I assure you that my heart is with you and I will journey to you as soon as possible. I wrote a long letter to the entire group, but I wish I were speaking to them personally, especially considering their lack of a preacher. This also motivates me to come to you quickly. I have great affection for you, and if I thought you had doubted that, I would write all the more words telling you the same.

May the Lord you trust guide and protect you and show you salvation, bringing us all together if he wills.

In Christ's name, Amen.

Yours,
John Robinson

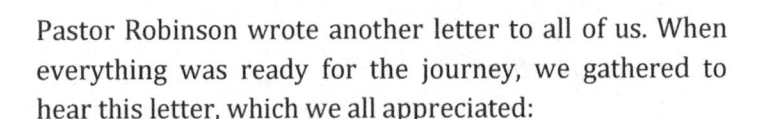

Pastor Robinson wrote another letter to all of us. When everything was ready for the journey, we gathered to hear this letter, which we all appreciated:

Loving Christian friends,

I greet you all in the Lord. Though I am far from you, my heart is with you. God knows how much I was willing to go with you on this journey. I am painfully divided within, wanting to be with you, but needing to remain here. And though I have no doubt that, in your godly wisdom, you understand your own present needs, I believe I owe you some helpful instruction.

As you know, we must daily approach God to repent of both our known and unknown sins. It is even more important, however, to carefully examine your ways during difficult times, so God will have no reason to judge you nor abandon you in the midst of danger due to some sin you've forgotten or did not make right. However, if you do repent of your sins and receive the Lord's pardon, he will grant you security and peace in all danger, comfort in all distress, and deliverance from all evil in both life and death.

Once we have peace with God and our own conscience, we must be careful to be at peace with all men, as much as it depends upon us (Rom. 12:8), especially with our friends. Be careful not to offend others, nor be easily offended by others. As Christ said regarding Satan's malice and man's corruption, "Woe to the world because of their offenses. For such things will happen, but woe to the person by whom the offense comes" (Matt. 18:7). If the Apostle Paul says that he would rather die than unwittingly offend others (1Cor. 9:15), it must be an even greater evil to intentionally disregard God and our love for man.

It is not enough to keep ourselves from offending; we must also guard against being easily offended. If someone does not have the love which "shall cover a multitude of sins" (1Pet. 4:8), evidently the work of grace is weak in that person. Those who are easily offended either lack the love that covers over other's mistakes, or they lack the wisdom to understand human imperfections, or perhaps they are like the hypocrites that the Lord warns us about (Matt. 7:1-3). In my experience I have found that it is more likely for people to *be easily offended, than to offend others.*

There are several reasons to be careful in these matters:

First, you are unfamiliar with each other and one another's weaknesses, so be careful not to be affected by other's unknown problems. It requires much love and wisdom to both prevent and forgive these kinds of offenses.

Unfortunately, the way you organize your community will offer many opportunities for conflict. It will be like fuel for the fire, therefore douse it with brotherly patience.

And if we must beware of becoming easily irritated with each other, we should be all the more careful not to become irritated with God himself, such as when we complain about the circumstances he brings our way. Therefore, store up patience for the day you need it, for without it we may get offended at the Lord himself in how he deals with us.

Fourth, keep a common concern for the whole community and shun the temptation of selfish comforts and personal advantages. Fight against selfish desires and any indifference for the common good of all others. Just as we are careful not to bump and jostle a new house before it is firmly built, I beg you brothers to be even more careful not to be shaken by problems and conflicts in this crucial time, for you are the house of God (2Cor. 6:16).

Finally, since you are forming a new community with a civil government, use wisdom and godliness as you choose leaders. Select those who are loving and will seek the good of all. Honor and obey those that govern. Do not treat them as ordinary citizens, but as God's administrators for your good (Rom. 13:1-4). Do not be like the foolish crowds who are more impressed with a person's fancy coat than with a virtuous mind or godly management (James 2:1-4). You know better than that, and you know the honor and authority that an official carries. I know you will willingly honor your leaders, because you yourselves will select them.

I could address other important issues, or say more about those I've discussed here, but I will not insult you by assuming you are unwise about these things. Besides, there are already those among you who are quite able to guide you.

Therefore, I leave these few words to your care and conscience, adding my constant daily prayers for you. May the God who made the heavens and earth and seas, and who guides all of his creation—especially his children—may he guide and guard you in all your ways, both inwardly by his Spirit and outwardly by his power. May this be so that we may all praise his name all the days of our lives. May you fare well in him in whom you trust and in whom I rest.

A true well-wisher of your happy success in this hopeful voyage,

John Robinson

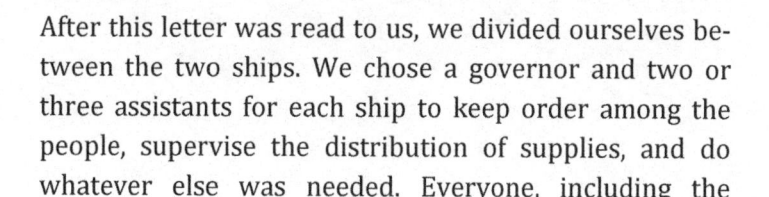

After this letter was read to us, we divided ourselves between the two ships. We chose a governor and two or three assistants for each ship to keep order among the people, supervise the distribution of supplies, and do whatever else was needed. Everyone, including the shipmasters, approved of this organization.

We set sail about August 5th, 1620. What happened to us next, further up the English coast, I will reveal in the next chapter.

The profile of a typical merchant ship, such as the *Mayflower*, of the early 1600s. Such ships were measured by their cargo space. The *Mayflower* was a 180 ton ship, meaning it could carry 180 standard-sized barrels within the cargo hold.

QUESTIONS FOR REFLECTION AND DISCUSSION:

1. As they left for London to prepare for their voyage, Bradford says that he and the Separatists "knew that we were pilgrims." Considering the context of his statement, what do you think he meant?

2. Who are the pilgrims of our day, and in what ways might we all be pilgrims?

3. Bradford describes the heartbreaking conversations between the Pilgrims and those who remained in Holland, knowing they may never see each other again. What would be the most important words you would share on such an occasion?

4. What were the Pilgrims' main complaints against the Merchant Adventurers Company that was financing their voyage and settlement?

5. Describe the promises and compromises the Pilgrims made to help satisfy their investors.

6. What do you think were the most important instructions of Pastor John Robinson in his last letter?

CHAPTER 8

Our Journey Delays

Sabotage and Endless Repairs
August - September 1620

WE DID NOT SAIL far before Captain Reynolds found a serious leak in the *Speedwell* that he said must be repaired. He and Captain Jones of the *Mayflower* decided to put in at Dartmouth, along England's southwest coast. There they inspected the small ship from stem to stern. They found the leaks, mended them, and the workmen reported that she was seaworthy once again.

We lost much time and some good wind, but we set off hoping there would be no more delays. We were disappointed. About three hundred miles out, the ship began to leak so much that the captain knew it would sink. We could not pump the water out fast enough. Both captains decided it was best to sail back to Plymouth in Devonshire as quickly as possible for more repairs.

This time, however, they found no serious leak. They concluded that the *Speedwell* was just not strong enough for the voyage. We were forced to leave the ship, along with many of our people, behind. We were heartbroken. The rest of us would cross the Atlantic on the *Mayflower* alone.

We believed she was large enough to carry more passengers and freight, so we stowed as much of the *Speedwell's* supplies as we could onto the *Mayflower*. We had to make the painful decisions of which supplies and passengers to leave behind. Some of our people were already reluctant to sail anyway, fearing the dangers of the journey. Others chose to remain because of their weak health. Some claimed it was far too late in the year for such a voyage, and even more chose to stay for the sake of their many young children.

Like the army of Gideon, our small company was divided as if the Lord himself determined that even those few were just too many for the work he had planned.[13] Therefore, there was yet another sad and final farewell as some of us returned to London, and the rest of us boarded the *Mayflower* to cross the Atlantic.

The Captain's Treachery

Much later we had learned that the problems with the *Speedwell* had less to do with structural weakness and more to do with treachery. A conspiracy was discovered

---

[13] Judges 7:2-8.

involving the captain himself and his crew. Sometime after our voyage, others had overheard the sailors themselves admitting that they and Captain Reynolds wanted out of their one year agreement with us. They feared they would die of starvation in the New Land, so to free themselves of their commitment they created a cunning plan to force the ship to leak.

The original mast of the *Speedwell* was replaced with one that was too big for the hull, and this was not by accident. When the sails were full, the heavy mast would lean, opening cracks in the hull and bringing in water. In fact, when she was later sold and fitted with her correct masts and sails, she made many successful voyages, performing well.

When we left Leiden, we first boarded the *Speedwell* in great appreciation of the captain and crew. But despite our show of gratitude, Captain Reynolds gave in to his fear and self-interest. He disregarded his duty, treated our kindness with contempt, and successfully carried out his deception, freeing himself of his obligation to us.

The Fears of Robert Cushman

It was while in port at Plymouth that Robert Cushman decided that he and his family would no longer sail with us, but would instead remain in England. It was not the first time his enthusiasm for our project had failed. As the *Speedwell* was being repaired back in Dartmouth, he openly confessed his grave doubts about the voyage in a letter to a friend.

Though his words reveal a fearful heart, Mr. Cushman later became a faithful friend and brother to us all in the New Land. Here is the letter of Robert Cushman:

Dartmouth
August 17, 1620

To Edward Southworth
Heneage House, Duke's Place, London, England

Loving friend,

My most kind thoughts go to you, your wife, dearest E.M., and others. I may never see you again in this life. Along with the deadly dangers of the voyage, a serious illness has attacked me and may not leave until it kills me. I have no idea what it is, but for two weeks my heart feels like it is being crushed beneath a load of lead. And though I feel like a walking dead man, I say let God's will be done.

This voyage has had so many troubles. We may have been halfway to Virginia now if it was not for our constantly leaking ship. We put in here at Dartmouth for repairs. Just three or four more hours at sea and we likely would have sunk. It was fixed twice at Southampton, but is now leaking like a sieve. Water was gushing in like a broken dike. There was a two foot board that was so loose you could pry it off with your fingers.

Earlier, as we waited for repairs in Southampton, seven days of good sailing weather passed us by, and now again we wait for the ship. Four more days of good winds have come and gone; it will likely be four more before we leave. By that time the wind will probably change for the worse as it did in Southampton.

Our food supplies will probably be half eaten before we leave the English coast, and if it's a long voyage, then the food will not even last a month after we finally land. We have spent nearly seven hundred pounds at Southampton. On what, I don't know. When we ask Christopher Martin, one of the leaders in our voyage, exactly how the money was spent, he gives us no clear answer. He instead becomes defensive, accusing us of being suspicious and ungrateful for all his trouble. It would break your heart to see how cruel and insulting he is to the poorer people, as if they were not even good enough to wipe his shoes.

I tried to talk to him, but he erupts in angry outbursts and accuses me of insubordination, refusing to listen to any complaints. He claims the people are merely demanding and ungrateful and I should not listen to their accusations.

Some people here are willing to give up everything they had invested in this effort if they could only return to shore, but he refuses to let them. Even the sailors are so tired of Mr. Martin controlling everything that some are threatening to either harm him or abandon the entire voyage. He is making a fool of himself.

Mr. Weston is another matter. He is furious that we did not approve the amended contract. He and his partners now blame Pastor Robinson for telling everyone to reject the new conditions. Mr. Weston also complains that it was his company that was given the authority to choose the leaders for our voyage—not us. Someday they will regret their actions.

It looked like everything would fall through back at Southampton if we did not agree to the new terms. It would have been better to cancel the whole voyage than to agree to such miserable, harmful conditions. In fact, at least four or five of the leaders from Leiden were determined not to sign the new agreement. Mr. Martin said he received no money based on the new conditions, and that he was not obligated one bit to those bloodsucking Merchant Adventurers. He himself made no agreement with the merchants, he said, nor did he even speak with them.

However, regarding all the money that Mr. Martin was in charge of, we still don't know where it all went. How can someone spend so much of other people's money and not be accountable for it? Furthermore, I fully informed him of the altered agreement and our obligations to the investors a long time ago and it was completely fine with him, but then later he accuses me of betraying everyone and making us all into slaves. He even claims that he could have prepared both ships himself with no help from the Merchant Adventurers. How could he do that? He only has fifty English pounds invested in the whole voyage!

Friend, if we actually do form a plantation it will be a miracle. We will have so little food left when we arrive. We are so divided among ourselves; we have no strong leaders. Violence will likely erupt. Where is the meek and humble spirit of Moses (Exod. 3:9-11), or even Nehemiah who led the people to rebuild the walls of Jerusalem and of Israel (Neh. 5:14-19)? Instead we have nothing but continual boasting like that of Rehoboam (1Kings 12:6-19). As the philosophers and wise men have always taught, harsh leaders will either bring themselves or their people down in ruins.

If I actually listed for you of all the signs of our eventual ruin it would be too much for the both of us. But I tell you this much only to prepare you for whatever bad news you may soon hear about us. Urgently pray for us! Perhaps the Lord can be swayed to help us.

I see no way we can ever escape the dying gasps of

starving people, but God can do much, and may his will be done. I would rather die right now than go through these struggles every day. And I am so sick both inside and out that I may die at any hour.

My poor friend William Ring and I both wonder who will first become food for the fishes, but we both look forward to our glorious resurrection. No longer will we know Christ Jesus in only our earthly bodies. Looking to the joy set before us, we will endure these sufferings (Heb. 12:2), and consider them light in comparison to the joy that we hope for (Rom. 18:8).

Please tell all our dear friends to pray for me, and that I hope to see them again in comfort. May the Lord give us the true comfort that no one can take away.

I intended this letter to be shorter, but I know you will understand why I needed to share all of this with you. Everything I have written is true and I could have written far more of the same.

I'm writing these words as if they were my last. You may share or conceal whatever you wish in this letter.

Forgive me. Both my head and body are weak.

May the Lord strengthen me, and protect both you and yours.

Your loving friend,
Robert Cushman

While we waited in Dartmouth for repairs, these were the thoughts and fears of Mr. Cushman which must have grown worse after we were forced to return to Plymouth in Devonshire.

QUESTIONS FOR REFLECTION AND DISCUSSION:

1. The *Speedwell* could not cross the Atlantic, which explains why the *Mayflower* became so crowded. If your loved ones had signed on for this journey, would you recommend that they continue the voyage at that point or stay behind? Why?

2. Bradford later heard that Captain Reynolds sabotaged the *Speedwell* so he would not have to stay in America with the Pilgrims for his one year agreement. Why do you think the captain did not attempt to get out of his contract honestly?

3. Both Bradford and Robert Cushman spell out the kinds of delays for their voyage. Should they have interpreted those delays as "signs" that they should not sail? Explain.

4. Recount the concerns that Cushman and others had with Christopher Martin. How would you deal with such a person under those circumstances?

5. Cushman uses several Biblical references to describe their experiences, which indicates that he saw their lives as part of a much bigger story. How is your life part of a larger story, and what kind of story is it?

CHAPTER 9

Dangerous Crossing

Our Two Months at Sea
September - November 1620

AFTER WE ALL BOARDED the *Mayflower*, we again put out to sea on the 6th of September. There was a good wind for several straight days, which was encouraging. As usual, many became seasick.

There was a special work of God which occurred on the seas. A strong, proud, and profane young sailor ridiculed the sick passengers, cursing at them daily. He said that he hoped half of us would die so that he could help toss our bodies overboard before the end of the voyage. If anyone even tried to gently correct him, he angrily cursed all the more.

Before we were halfway across the ocean, however, God had struck the man with a terrible disease, and so the young sailor died. He himself became the first to be tossed overboard. His fellow crewmen were shocked that his own curse came upon himself, and they all knew it was the punishment of God.

After a period of pleasant wind and weather, we were hit by crosswinds and storms so fierce that it shook the vessel, creating leaks in the upper deck. The main beam had bent—then cracked!

Passengers overheard crewmen muttering among themselves about whether the ship was strong enough to finish the voyage. As the winds died down, some of our leaders met with the captain and his officers about returning to England instead of endangering ourselves any further. Even the sailors were divided. Since we were half way across the ocean, some wanted to continue so they could be paid for the voyage, while others did not want to risk their lives in a damaged ship.

Captain Jones and others believed the ship was secure beneath the water line. As for the broken deck beam, the passengers had a solution. We brought with us a huge iron jackscrew from Holland. Using it, we were able to force the beam back into place. When that was done, a post was put tightly beneath it in the lower deck, making it strong enough to complete the voyage. The upper decks were caulked sufficiently and would remain sealed if they carefully watched the strain on the sails. When we were finished, we again committed ourselves to the will of God and resolved to continue.

Some of the storms were so fierce and the waves so high that we couldn't let the sails out even one knot. For several days we were forced to let the sea carry us wherever it will. In one such storm, John Howland, a healthy

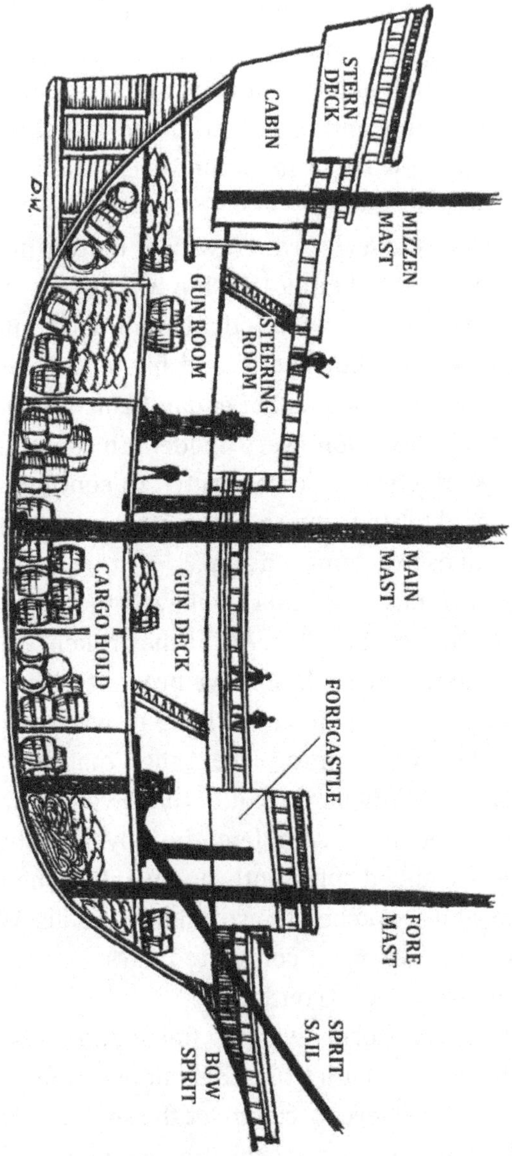
STERN DECK
CABIN
MIZZEN MAST
GUN ROOM
STEERING ROOM
MAIN MAST
GUN DECK
CARGO HOLD
FORECASTLE
FORE MAST
SPRIT SAIL
BOW SPRIT
D.W.

young man, went to the upper deck where he was thrown into the sea. He clutched a halyard rope hanging overboard. Even underwater, John held tight. They pulled him until finally his head came above water. They grabbed him with a boat hook and yanked him back up on deck, saving his life. Though the experience left him ill, John lived many years, growing into an important member of our church and community.

Arriving at the New World

After a two-month beating from the sea, we finally sighted Cape Cod. We were thrilled! Only one passenger was lost during the entire voyage. Young William Button, a servant to Samuel Fuller, died as we neared the coast.

We turned south to find a place to settle near the Hudson River. The wind and weather were fair. Around midday we sailed into dangerously shallow water and nearly ran aground in the rocks. The wind began to die down. We turned the ship north again toward the cape and with God's help we managed to leave there before nightfall.

The next day we safely sailed into the harbor of Cape Cod, so named by Captain Gosnold in 1602. We named the shoals "Point Care" or "Tucker's Terror" where we nearly ran aground. Because of the losses suffered there, the French call it "Malabar."

Safely in the harbor, some of us took out the ship's rowboat and headed for shore. When we stepped onto land, we fell down upon our knees thanking the God of heaven who brought us over this vast, furious ocean. The ancient Roman philosopher Seneca had once said that he would rather travel twenty years over land than even a short time over the sea. But God had now delivered us from all those dangers and miseries to set our feet once again upon solid earth. We were overjoyed!

Though we survived such a sea of trouble that began before we even set sail, and we finally crossed the vast ocean, we now had no friends to welcome us. There were no towns, no houses, and no inns to refresh our weather-beaten bodies. Nothing.

The Scriptures tell us the Apostle Paul and his fellow travelers were shown kindness by the barbarians of Malta when their ship ran aground,[14] but the savage barbarians we would later meet were more likely to fill our sides full of arrows. It was a hideous and desolate wilderness which greeted us, full of wild beasts and wild men.

Summer was far gone. Winter had already arrived, and winter here is sharp and violent, prone to fierce storms. Traveling becomes dangerous, even when going to familiar places.

Unlike Moses who could see the Promised Land laid out before him from atop Mount Pisgah,[15] we had no such view that would feed our hopes or give us comfort. This whole country, full of woods and thickets, was a wild and savage sight. The mighty ocean behind us became a great chasm, separating us from the entire civilized world.

---

[14] Acts 28:1-2.
[15] Deuteronomy 3:27.

Every day the captain and crew urged us to hurry, telling us to take out their rowboat to find a place nearby to settle. The captain said he would not bring the ship in any closer this time of year unless he was certain it was a safe harbor. He also warned us that their food supplies were dwindling, and he must reserve enough for the crew's return voyage. Some crew members even muttered that if we did not find a place soon enough that they would merely dump both us and our belongings on the shore and abandon us there.

Considering how we and our investors had parted, we had little reason to expect help from them anytime soon. Though our friends in Leiden dearly loved us, they had little means to send us any aid. Only the Spirit and grace of God could help us now.

Our children will later say of us, "Our fathers were Englishmen who came over this great ocean, and were close to dying in this wilderness. 'But then they cried out to the Lord, and he heard their voice and delivered them from their distress. Praise the Lord, for he is good. His mercy endures forever. Let the redeemed of the Lord tell how he has delivered them from the hand of the enemy. They wandered alone in the desert wilderness and found no city to dwell in. They were hungry and thirsty, their souls fainted within them. Let them praise the Lord for his loving-kindness and his wonderful works for the children of men'."[16]

---

[16] Psalms 107:1-8.

QUESTIONS FOR REFLECTION AND DISCUSSION:

1. Why did both the Pilgrims and the *Mayflower* crew interpret the young sailor's death as God's punishment? How might that incident impact the difficult relationship between the religious Pilgrims and salty sailors?

2. The iron jackscrew they used to repair the ship's deck was likely brought to help with construction. Halfway across the ocean, if the Pilgrims did not have that tool, would you have voted to continue across the Atlantic or return home, and why?

3. Explain what happened to John Howland. How do you think that experience impacted the rest of his life in the New World?

4. What were Bradford's concerns when they finally reached Cape Cod, and which of those concerns would worry you the most?

5. Why did the *Mayflower*'s captain pressure the Pilgrims to hurry and find a place to settle? Explain whether you think he was right or wrong in doing so.

CHAPTER 10

Finding a Home

The Search for a Place to Settle
November - December 1620

WE LANDED AT CAPE COD on November 11. The *Mayflower* crew insisted we begin our search for a place to live, so we soon took out our shallop that was stored within the ship. But as we began to prepare it for sailing we discovered the great damage it suffered in the rough voyage. Despite the dangers, some men insisted that we explore the area on foot as others repaired the shallop, so Captain Standish chose sixteen armed men to go ashore.

We set out with Captain Jones' rowboat on the 15th of November. Once on land, we marched only about a mile along the shore before we saw five or six savages and a dog approaching in the distance. They spotted us, then turned and fled into the woods. We followed, hoping to speak with them or at least find out if there were more waiting in ambush for us. When they saw us following, they ran toward the beach. We tracked their footprints in the sand for miles, but we could never catch up.

Evening came upon us, so we appointed guards and rested for the night. The next morning we continued tracking the Indians. Their footprints led to a creek near the woods. We tried to find where they lived, but not only did we lose the Indians, we lost ourselves as well. The thickets tore at our clothing, and we became thirsty.

Finally we came upon fresh water. It was our first taste of the waters of New England, and in our great thirst it was as good as the wine of days gone by. Then we marched across the narrow strip of land back to shore, finding a large pond of fresh, clear water.

What They Found

Along the way we came across vast stubbly acres of old Indian cornfields, perfect for plowing. We also discovered the remains of a house, with cut wooden planks and a large iron kettle nearby. And then there were the graves.

A far more lovely sight, however, was what we uncovered beneath some heaps of sand—baskets filled with seed corn and full ears of beautiful, multi-colored corn such as we had never seen before. All this we found near the mouth of the saltwater river which opened into the bay, two arms of water spreading north and south. It looked to be a good harbor for our shallop. A high sandy cliff loomed near the entrance.

With time growing short, we returned to the safety of

the ship. Just as the Hebrew scouts brought to Moses a sampling of fruit from the promise land, gladdening the hearts of the wanderers,[17] so we too returned to our ship with a heavy load of corn to encourage the hearts of those on board.

When our shallop was finally repaired, Captain Jones himself took some thirty men to examine the New Land. We found suitable harbors for smaller boats, but not for the *Mayflower*.

We discovered two Indian dwellings with matted roofs and tools within, but people were nowhere to be found. We also came upon more corn and various colored beans which we brought back with us, intending to fully repay the Indians when we could. (In fact, six months later, we did indeed repay the Indians to their satisfaction.)

It was nothing less than the merciful provision of God that we found the seed corn to plant for the coming year, for soon the ground was so frozen and covered with snow that it would have been impossible to discover the corn later. We probably would have starved without it. The Lord will always be there for his own when they are in greatest need. Praise his holy name!

Those were the tasks which consumed us in November. But on the 6th of December, with the cold of winter approaching us, ten of our leaders and some crewmen took out the shallop to explore further. We circled about Cape Cod, with the sea spray freezing upon our coats, encasing us in a thick glaze of ice.

---

[17] Numbers 13:17-27.

Come evening, we sailed into the south bay. As we drew near the shore, we spied about a dozen Indians busy about something, so we chose to land a few miles away. We had difficulty putting ashore anywhere because the water was so shallow.

Later, after we landed, we gathered logs and branches and put together the best fort we could in a short time. One man stood guard as the others slept. He watched the smoke rise from the savages' fire in the distance.

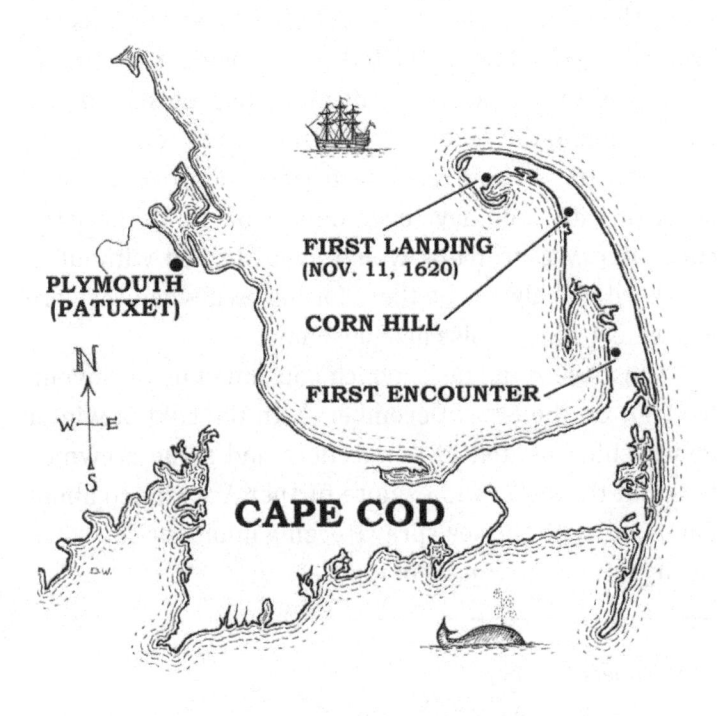

When morning came we divided into two groups. Some took the boat along the shore as the rest of us marched through the woods, looking for suitable land. We came to the site where we spied the Indians just the night before. There we found the remains of a huge fish, with a layer of fat two inches thick like a hog. Pieces were strewn about. Those in the boat found two more of these fish dead upon the sands. Apparently they often become stranded upon the mudflats after a storm.

Those of us on land marched up and down all day and found no people, nor any place suitable to build. The sun grew low and we hurried out of the woods to meet up with the boat. When we spotted it we motioned for them to approach a nearby creek at high tide. We were all glad to be reunited; our two groups had not seen each other since morning.

Using logs, sticks, and thick pine boughs as tall as a man, we quickly built another barricade, as we came to do every evening, protecting ourselves from the chilling wind and any surprise attack from savages. After that we gathered about the fire, cold and exhausted, and we slept.

The Frightening Encounter

About midnight there was a loud and hideous cry. The sentry called out, "Weapons! Get your weapons!" We grabbed our muskets and sprang to our feet. One fired, and then another. Then the noise ceased. Wolves or wild beasts, we presumed. One of the sailors said he often heard such cries in Newfoundland.

At about five in the morning we were awakened by the tides. The day was dawning and there was much to do, so after morning prayer we began carrying our belongings down to the shallop and prepare for breakfast.

Our muskets were lying down, wrapped in our coats to keep them dry, but there was disagreement about the weapons. Some men stored their guns in the shallop. A few others said they would keep their firearms nearby until the tide was high enough to sail, so these men laid their weapons on the bank and came up for breakfast.

Suddenly there were loud screams in the distance—the same eerie voices we heard at night. One of our men came running. "Indians, men! Indians!" Arrows flew in. By God's grace the men quickly grabbed their muskets, but only four of us had our firearms with us. Two men fired. The others were commanded to hold fire until they had a clear shot.

Those who left their firearms at the boat quickly put on the chain armor. They grabbed their swords and ran to the shallop as the others defended the barricade. When the Indians saw the men running, they let out a bone-chilling scream and fired upon them. The men grabbed their guns and then fired back. The Indians abruptly ceased their attack—all but one, that is.

One ruggedly fierce Indian stood behind a tree and kept firing upon us. He was within easy range of our muskets. Three shots missed him. One man carefully aimed his musket and fired again, hitting the tree just beside the Indian. Bark and tree splinters flew about his ears. He gave a loud shriek, and then they all fled away.

We decided it was best to show the Indians we were not intimidated, so leaving a few men to guard the shallop, we followed the Indians about a quarter mile. We shouted and fired our guns, and then returned.

God had delivered us. We defeated our enemies. Despite the arrows raining upon us, by God's divine care not a one of us was scratched. When we returned to the barricade we found several of our coats still hanging there, pierced through with arrows. We named that spot the "Place of First Encounter."

We offered to God a solemn prayer of gratitude for our deliverance. We gathered arrows to send back to England with the ship captain.

Fighting a Deadly Storm

From there we sailed the shallop along the coast. We still found no place deep enough to bring in the ship, and the weather was growing worse. Mr. Robert Coppin, one of the ship's pilots, was with us. He had sailed these waters before, and we were all relieved when he said there was a suitable harbor we could reach before nightfall.

We sailed our shallop for hours, rain and snow coming down on us. By midafternoon a storm was brewing. The winds beat upon us. The waves grew fierce, twisting the boat. The rudder broke off. Two men quickly strained at the oars to steer the boat, fighting against the storm.

"Hang on, men!" Mr. Coppin shouted. "I see the harbor!" But the storm grew worse. Night was looming, and in the fading light we struggled to sail ashore. A powerful gust slammed against us and shattered our mast to pieces. The sail fell into the swelling sea; our hearts sank.

By God's mercy we finally reclaimed control of the shallop, and the tide began pulling us toward the harbor.

Yet when we came closer, our joy turned to dread. "God have mercy!" Mr. Coppin cried. "My eyes tricked me! This is not the place! It is not the harbor!"

The wind pushed us toward the breakers. We were about to run aground. One rugged sailor, struggling to control the shallop, shouted to those at the oars, "If you are truly men, then turn this around or we will wreck!" When we turned her around, the sailor said, "Good work, men, and keep rowing!"

Thankfully we were moving into deeper waters, and Mr. Coppin was certain we would find safer passage. The sky was dark. The rain poured. We finally reached a safe place to land, shielded from the wind. Some wanted to

A shallop was a small sailboat that could also be rowed, if needed.

stay in the boat in case the Indians came, but others were so weak, drenched and frozen, they needed immediate shelter. We gladly went ashore and remained there in safety all through the night. As we slept, the wind shifted to the northwest, freezing everything.

The day before was one of trouble and danger, yet we awoke to a gift of God—a morning of comfort and refreshing. We were on an island, safe from the Indians. It was a glorious day of sunshine. That day we dried our clothing, attended our firearms, rested our bodies, and gave thanks to our merciful God for delivering us time and time again. This is what God does for his children. Since it was the last day of the week, we prepared to stay there for a day of worship on Sunday.

When Monday came we checked the harbor's depth and found it deep enough to bring in the *Mayflower*. We marched inland and discovered cornfields, tiny streams, and—most important—a place to settle. It was the best place we could find, and with winter approaching, it would be good enough. We went back to the ship and shared the news, and everyone was happy and relieved.

[Dear reader, please forgive my intrusion into William Bradford's journal, but at this point in the story there is a crucial and painful event he does not share with you. On Tuesday, the 12th of December, Mr. Bradford and the men in the shallop made it back to the *Mayflower* to report that they had finally found an acceptable place to settle. But whatever joy that news provided, it was surely overshadowed by what had happened earlier, for when they returned to the ship, Mr. Bradford was told that just five days before his dear wife Dorothy had fallen over the side and drowned in the cold harbor of Cape Cod. Many today believe it could have been suicide, which may explain why Mr. Bradford does not speak at all of the event—so painful it was for him. Whatever had happened, from this point on all the rest of his experiences in the New World would occur without the companionship of his wife. - D.W.]

On the 15th of December Captain Jones ordered that the anchor be brought up, and we began to sail toward our new home. The winds grew stronger, so we stayed about six miles from shore during the night. The next day the winds were calm and we sailed safely into harbor. After reviewing the area, we decided where we should build. And on the 25th of December we began constructing our common house to securely store our goods and to shelter our people.

QUESTIONS FOR REFLECTION AND DISCUSSION:

1. When the Pilgrim men came upon the Indian's corn, they felt pulled between the two competing values of honor and providing for their families. What do you think about their choice? Were there other alternatives?

2. They discovered what seemed to be the remains of a European style house as evidenced by the cut wooden planks and the iron kettle. What scenarios can you think of that might explain their discovery?

3. In this chapter we find the Pilgrims searching for a suitable place to construct a settlement. In choosing a site, what kinds of things would they be looking for?

4. We sense the fear of the settlers as Bradford talks about the skirmish on the beach, but what do you think the Native Americans were feeling and thinking then?

5. What possible reasons might explain why Governor Bradford never mentions his wife, or her tragic death?

CHAPTER 11

The Sickness

How Half Our Number Died
1620 - 1621

ALLOW ME TO GO BACK to events that occurred six weeks ago while we were all yet aboard ship. There was a heated debate about the original agreement that we settlers made regarding the rules that would govern us in the New Land. Discontented and mutinous speeches spewed forth from some who made the journey with us yet were not part of our church. These "strangers" told us that when they go ashore, they will do as they please and answer to no one.

They argued that our legal agreement with the Virginia Company of London pertained explicitly to the area of Virginia, and since we were now settling even further north, then they were no longer bound by that agreement. Under the circumstances we all decided that a new agreement, one which we ourselves created, would be just as binding as any other. Here is that new agreement:

> We, whose names are written below, are the loyal subjects of King James—our mighty supreme Lord, ruler of Great Britain, France, and Ireland, and defender of the Christian faith by the grace of God.
>
> We have undertaken a voyage to plant the first colony in the parts north of Virginia for the glory of God, the advancement of the Christian faith, and the honor of king and country.
>
> In the presence of God and one another, we do now solemnly and mutually covenant and combine ourselves together into a civil political body to better arrange, preserve, and further these goals.
>
> This we do to create fair and impartial laws and authorities for the general good of the Colony as our situation demands, and we do hereby promise to obey these laws.
>
> In the name of God, Amen.
>
> In acknowledgment of this agreement, we hereby sign our names at Cape Cod on November 11, 1620.

After we had signed the agreement, we chose Mr. John Carver, a well-respected and godly man, to serve as our first governor.

We finished the common house for our supplies, and began building our cottages. Unloading the ship was a long and difficult work due to the lack of boats, the foul winter weather, and the illnesses plaguing our people.

As time allowed and circumstances demanded, we met to discuss the laws and regulations which would govern our community and civil defense, making any changes that the situation required.

During these most difficult times we were informed of discontented grumblings and treacherous plots. They were soon quelled, however, by the wise and just manner of our governor and the pressure put upon them by the majority, who usually stick together.

Over the next few months, half our people died. Where there were once over one hundred of us, now there were barely fifty. January and February were the worst. Weakened by the long, grueling journey, we were ravaged by scurvy and other diseases. Between illness, the freezing cold, and the lack of sufficient shelter, sometimes two or three of us died every day.

In the worst of it there were only six or seven people strong enough at any one time to look after the rest. Night and day they toiled, risking their health, fetching wood, building fires, preparing meals, making up beds, dressing the sick, and washing our loathsome clothes. They did all the revolting tasks that more dainty and squeamish souls would never even speak of, and they did it willingly and cheerfully.

They showed a true love toward their friends and brothers, a rare example today worthy to be remembered. Among those who served the sick and dying were our church elder William Brewster and Myles Standish, our military captain. We owe them our lives. The Lord kept them from illness so they could serve the rest of us.

The same charity we had seen in these men was even seen in those who had died in the scourge. If they had any strength at all, they continued to care for those who needed them. Their reward is now with the Lord; I have no doubt.

Our character was far different from the ship's crew. Thirsty and overcome with sickness, I requested just a cup of beer from one of the sailors. He said, "Not even if you were my own father!" These were the sailors who hurried us off the ship to find water so they may have the rest of the beer to themselves.

The Sickness Spread Further

The illness came upon the crew and nearly half of them also died before they sailed home. Officers, a gunner, a cook, and many of their strongest men were not spared. When the captain himself became ill, he sent word to our governor that our sick could have some of their beer if they needed it, even if the crew had to drink water on their journey home.

Along with the afflictions that the ship's crew endured, another miserable disease emerged: indifference. Sailors who were once jolly drinking companions when they were healthy later abandoned each other in this calamity. They were not about to risk their own lives by entering the cabins of their sick fellow crewmen. "So, if they are going to die," they said, "then let them die!"

Some passengers who were still onboard gave these forsaken men what aid they could, softening the hearts of some of them. There was one proud man, a young officer, who cursed and mocked us upon the sea, but when he too fell ill our people were there to show compassion. Mindful of his contemptible behavior toward us, he was bewildered at our kindness. Feeling ashamed, he confessed, "You people show your Christian love to one another, yet we seamen let each other die like dogs."

One miserable soul lay cursing his wife, saying he would never have come on this doomed voyage if it were not for her. He went on to curse his shipmates, complaining that after all he had done for them and all the money he had spent upon them, they will now have nothing to do with him in his greatest time of need.

Another man pledged to give a shipmate all of his belongings upon his death if only he would look after him in his misery. The sailor prepared some spices and one or two meals for the man. However, when the poor wretch did not soon die, the man swore to his companions that the rogue was trying to cheat him out of what he had promised. "I would rather see him choke," he said, "before I give him one more meal." Before sunrise, the poor soul was gone.

The Indians Came

As our people were sick and dying, the Indians crept about. Sometimes they watched us from a distance, but if we ever approached them, they scattered. Once, after working on our cottages, we left for a meal only to return and find they had stolen our tools.

On the 16th of March a nearly naked savage boldly walked into our settlement. We were even more astonished when he spoke English. It was broken English, but we understood him. His name was Samoset, and he was a leader of a village further east. It was there he came into contact with English fishermen. He even listed the names of some of them.

The Indian carefully described this area and its natives for us, along with the size and location of Indian villages and the names of their chiefs. He also said there was an Indian named Squanto, a native of this place, who had actually been to England and could speak even better English than he could. We then fed Samoset and presented him with gifts. He remained for a night and left in the morning.

Sometime later Samoset returned with five more Indians—and our stolen tools. Soon, they said, their great chief would come, and four or five days later Chief Massasoit arrived.

He was a stern looking man with a chain of bones hanging about his neck. With him were many fearsome warriors, tall and strong, with painted faces. The Indian named Squanto came with them. We gave them food and drink and gifts, and with Squanto as our interpreter, we constructed a peace treaty together between the chief and our people.

1. Neither Chief Massasoit nor his people would do any harm to our people.

2. If any of his tribe harmed any of us, he would hand over the offender so we may punish him.

3. If anything of ours was taken by them, he would return it and we would do the same for him.

4. If anyone unjustly fought against him, we would come to their assistance; and if anyone fought against us, he would then assist us.

5. He would inform the leaders of his neighboring tribes of our treaty, so they also would not wrong us, but would cooperate in this agreement.

6. Finally, whenever their men come to visit us, they would leave their bows and arrows behind them.

Squanto and Mr. Dermer

After we made the agreement, Chief Massasoit and his warriors returned to his village called Sowams, forty miles away. Squanto, however, stayed with us. He was a special instrument sent from God, helping us beyond our expectations. He taught us how to plant corn, where to fish, and how to obtain other provisions. He was our interpreter, our guide about the land, and he stayed with us until the day he died.

Squanto was a native of the very place we landed, yet none of his people had been found alive. Years before, he and several others were kidnapped by Captain Thomas

A PLYMOUTH PILGRIM

The friendship of Chief Massasoit and the Wampanoags was crucial to the survival of the struggling Plymouth Colony.

Hunt, an Englishman who captured Indians to sell them in Spain as slaves. Some kind men, however, helped Squanto get to England where he worked for a London sea merchant. He became a guide and interpreter in Newfoundland and other parts, and finally returned home while under the employ of Mr. Thomas Dermer. Captain Dermer was an explorer and partner with Sir Ferdinando

Gorges, who had plans to profit from this land.

In 1622 Mr. Dermer's story was told in a book published by the President and Council of New England. He made peace between the English and the savages in these parts, which has helped our plantation to this day. That peace was rather weak, however, as can be seen in the fate of Mr. Dermer and his men.

According to a letter he wrote on June 30, 1620, Captain Dermer was in this very place just four months before we had arrived. Here is what Mr. Dermer wrote about this area:

> *I begin with the place called Plymouth on Captain John Smith's map, the very place from which Squanto (or Tisquantum) was taken. If only it had sufficient resources, I would prefer to begin the first plantation there if just fifty people would commit to the project. Otherwise, further north at Charlton would be good, for the savages are far less of a problem there. Just west of New Plymouth are the Pokanokets, which are continually hostile to the English and they are more numerous than all the savages from there to Penobscot combined.*
>
> *The Pokanokets still want revenge for the actions of one English seaman. After bringing many of them aboard his ship, they were all shot for apparently no reason, so the Indians claim. I question whether it was truly Englishmen, but the French have convinced them it was. The savages would have killed me at Namasket if it were not for Squanto pleading on my behalf.*
>
> *The soil around this large bay can be compared to most plantations I have seen in Virginia, with a variety of land. The area of Patuxet (which Smith calls Plym-*

outh) has a hardy but strong soil. The lands of Nauset and Satucket are mostly a blackish and deep mud, much like the best tobacco growing soil in Virginia. And in the bottom of the bay is a treasure of cod, bass, and mullet. But the Pokanoket area is best for the richest soil and vast open ground, perfect for English grain.

The area of Massachusetts is nearly thirty miles north from New Plymouth, and between them are countless fertile islands and peninsulas.

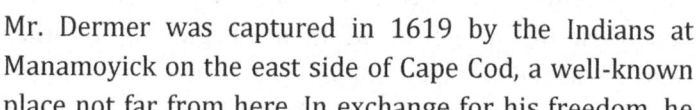

Mr. Dermer was captured in 1619 by the Indians at Manamoyick on the east side of Cape Cod, a well-known place not far from here. In exchange for his freedom, he conceded to their demands. But they still refused to release him and they planned to kill his men. Somehow he managed to get free, seizing some Indians, keeping them bound until they gave him a canoe filled with corn.[18]

After writing the letter above, Mr. Dermer and Squanto came to the Isle of Capawack, south toward Virginia. He went ashore to trade with the Indians, as he often did, but this time he was betrayed. He and his men were ambushed. Captain Dermer was wounded and all of his men were slaughtered—all of them except one sailor standing guard on the boat. Though seriously wounded, Mr. Dermer ran for the boat. The Indians would have chopped his head off in the boat's cabin if it had not been for that one sailor and his sword.

---

[18] Samuel Purchase, *Purchase His Pilgrims*, Vol 4 (1625), p. 1778.

And so they escaped, quickly sailing to the safety of Virginia, where Mr. Dermer later died. Whether it was from his wounds or the diseases of this place, it is not clear. But it is indeed clear how fragile the peace was here and how dangerous it was to begin our plantation in New Plymouth. The Lord, however, protects us by his mighty hand.

The Fate of the Frenchmen

These events were among the reasons why the Indians kept their distance from us in the beginning. Another reason was the Frenchmen.

Three years before we landed, a French vessel had shipwrecked at Cape Cod. The crewmen came ashore with ample food and supplies. The Indians learned about them and closely followed the sailors until they found an opportunity. All but three or four Frenchmen were slaughtered, and those few poor souls were kept alive merely for the cruel entertainment of the Indians, living worse than slaves, being sent back and forth between the various chiefs who abused them for sport.

It was Captain Dermer who purchased two of these men from the Indians and released them. This was another reason why the Indians here were afraid at first to make contact with us; they thought the *Mayflower* and its passengers had come to seek vengeance upon those who killed the Frenchmen.

In fact, before they came to befriend us, they told us that they had gathered all the medicine men of the area for a horrid and demonic three days of cursing us and conjuring spells against us, holding their evil ceremonies in a dark and dismal swamp.

Now I return to the arrival of our first spring in Plymouth Plantation. God was pleased to finally stop the dying that occurred all around us. He strengthened our sick and lame, which gave us new purpose and vigor. We endured our dreadful afflictions with as much peace and patience as anyone could muster, however it was the Lord who gave us the strength. Since childhood, God was already preparing many of us for this burden long before.

I will ignore many of the smaller issues. Some of those events are already published by one of our own men, along with other accounts and letters regarding our journey. Consult them if you wish to know more about the beginning of Plymouth Plantation.

Now I come to the 25th of March, 1621, and I will recount more of the events of that year.

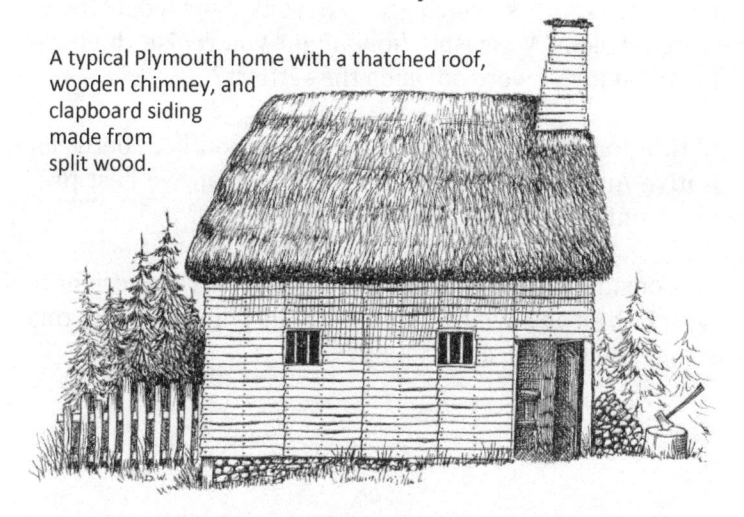

A typical Plymouth home with a thatched roof, wooden chimney, and clapboard siding made from split wood.

QUESTIONS FOR REFLECTION AND DISCUSSION:

1. Bradford said that the "strangers" refused to follow their agreement since they did not land in Virginia as they all planned. Were they justified in objecting to their agreed terms about the authority structure? Explain.

2. The "Mayflower Compact" that the passengers made on the ship is brief in view of its historical significance. What do you think are the most important aspects of it?

3. What might have happened to the *Mayflower* settlers if they all went their own way after they landed, seeking only their own welfare?

4. Compare the differences between the Pilgrims and the *Mayflower* crew when they all were plagued with illness. Why was there such a contrast between them?

5. Looking at the treaty between Chief Massasoit and the Plymouth settlers, which group does it favor most? If you were advising Massasoit, how might you revise the treaty? What if you were advising the settlers?

6. Bradford recites some of the tragic conflicts between Native Americans and Europeans. How can we best prevent conflict and violence between cultures?

7. Considering Squanto's horrifying past experiences with Europeans, why would he still be willing to help this struggling English community?

CHAPTER 12

Springtime to Harvest

Surviving Our First Year
March - November 1621

IT WAS AT THE END of March or beginning of April that we prepared to send the *Mayflower* and her crew back to England, leaving the rest of us here. The ship had already stayed much longer than anyone planned because we could not find a suitable harbor until last December.

It also took time for us to build our common house which we used for storage and for shelter as we built our cabins. But weeks later, on the 14th of January, we suffered another disaster. The common house burned down, and many of us had to stay in the ship yet again.

After all these events, then the sickness came. Disease spread about, taking the lives of many friends. The severe winter also fought against us, keeping us from settling upon the land.

With so many of our number devastated by sickness and death, and under constant danger of Indians, our leaders thought it best to keep the ship here until we built adequate shelter. With many already dead, it was far better to go deeper in debt for the ship than to risk death for the rest of us.

The crewmen had at first wanted to hurry us off the ship and be done with us so they could sail back to England. But then many of their own became sick and several of them died, even among their strongest, so they decided it was best to wait. Considering their condition, the captain dared not put to sea before his crew began to recover and the worst of winter had left. Then, on the 5th of April, the *Mayflower* and her crew finally sailed home.

Those of us who were healthy enough began to plant corn. Squanto was exceedingly valuable, teaching us how to plant and tend cornfields, and how to use fish to fertilize the seed as we planted in these old grounds. In mid-April the herring fish filled the brook that ran alongside the settlement. Squanto taught us how to catch them and gather other necessary provisions, and all his instructions proved true. Our wheat, peas, and other English seed were planted, but they did not flourish. Whether the problem was in the strength of the seed, the time of year, or some other reason, we don't know.

As we were busy planting on a hot day in April, Governor Carver trudged out of the fields very sick with a painful headache. He lay down and within a few hours he couldn't move, he couldn't speak. Days later, he died. Our hearts were broken; it was a terrible loss. We buried him with as much honor as we could, firing shots into the air. Five or six weeks later his wife Catherine, being a weak woman herself, also died.

After our dear friend left us, the community selected me to fill the position of governor. Since I was still recovering from the sickness that nearly took my life, they chose Mr. Isaac Allerton to assist me. Both of us were selected by an annual election for many years afterwards.

On May 12, 1621, Edward Winslow and Susanna White were married. Both of them lost their first spouses to the terrible sickness. It was the first marriage performed in our settlement, and it was a civil ceremony led by a governing official, for many legal issues depend upon it. This is the admirable manner in which they sealed marriages in Holland where we lived for a time, but more importantly it is consistent with the Christian faith. Nowhere in our Scriptures do we find the authority for ministers to conduct marriages. In fact the book of Ruth shows us the example of a marriage conducted as a civil affair, confirmed and witnessed by the town officials.[19]

Jean F. Le Petit says this law regarding marriage has been established in the Netherlands since 1590, and that no matter the religion, anyone desiring to be married must come before government officials.[20] And this has continued to be the practice of all notable Christian churches in our area up to this day.

---

[19] Ruth 4:5-15.
[20] Jean F. Le Petit, *A General History of the Netherlands*, trans. Edward Grimeston (1608-09), p. 1029.

Having made progress establishing our settlement, we decided it was time to visit our new friend Chief Massasoit to show our gratitude and strengthen our relationship with him. We were also curious about Massasoit's country—how he lived and also the population of his village—and we wanted to find the best route to his village if we needed it. On July 2, 1621, we sent Edward Winslow and Stephen Hopkins, with Squanto as their guide.

A Devastating Plague and the Kidnappings

They walked forty miles to Massasoit's village, and when they arrived they presented him with clothing, a horseman's coat, and other small gifts which he gratefully received. They had good soil there, but their village was small. Our men learned that great numbers of Massasoit's people died some three years earlier by a terrible plague brought here by Englishmen. Thousands had died, so many in fact that the living were no longer able to bury the dead. Countless Indian skulls and bones were scattered about in empty villages. It was a terribly sad sight.

Massasoit told them of the Narragansett Indians on the other side of the bay. They were a strong people, many in number, living close together, and untouched by the plague. Our men found little in common with Massasoit's people, however, and they returned home weary and hungry, for at that time the Indians had very little corn. Those were the days before the English supplied them with farming tools and showed the Indians how to prepare new ground.

Near the end of July, young John Billington vanished. I sent word to Chief Massasoit, asking about the boy. The frightening news came back that he was with the Nausets. These were the Indians that ambushed us on the shore, the very Indians whose corn reserves we had taken last winter. I quickly sent several of our men and Squanto out with the shallop to retrieve him.

After a stormy journey, they found the home of the Nausets. Crowds of armed Indians met them upon the shore. They brought the boy out unharmed. Our men then promised to them that we would pay for the corn we had taken, and so peace was established between our people and the Nausets.

Young John said he got lost in the woods, wandering about for five days, eating berries and anything he could find. He finally came upon an Indian village twenty miles south of our settlement. It was the Manomet tribe. But instead of returning him to us, they took him even further south to the Nausets.

These events served us well, giving us opportunity to create a good relationship with the Nausets. Now peace was settled between us and all the natives around our settlement. Hobomok, a trusted and proven warrior for Massasoit, came to live among us. He stayed with us as our faithful and constant friend until the day he died.

A frightening incident occurred in which both our Indian friends, Hobomok and Squanto, were in terrible danger. They were returning from doing business for us among the Indians when they were confronted by an Indian named Corbitant, fourteen miles west of us in the village of Namasket. He was an assistant chief to Massasoit, but has never been a friend to our people. Corbitant began arguing with them and pulled a knife, threatening to kill Hobomok.

Hobomok managed to flee, escaping to the safety of our village, but Squanto was left behind. Dripping with sweat, Hobomok told us that Corbitant threatened to kill them both for befriending and helping our people, and he feared that Squanto had already been killed.

We decided something had to be done. If we allowed our two Indian friends to suffer like this, no Indians would ever again run the risk of offering us help and friendship, and soon the hostile Indians would threaten us. We sent Captain Standish with a regiment of fourteen well-armed men to track down the Indians in the cover of night. If Squanto truly was killed, then they decided that they must find Corbitant and cut off his head. However, they would do no harm to any Indians who were innocent of Squanto's blood.

On the 14th of August, in the dark of night, Hobomok quietly guided our men into the Indian village. They surrounded Corbitant's hut, and posted guards. Captain Standish entered. Three Indians burst out of the hut. They were quickly shot by our guards. When the Captain searched inside, Corbitant was not there; but they learned that Squanto was still alive.

Our men did no other harm, and some frightened Indians came to speak with them. When Hobomok explained what our men were doing, the Indians brought out the best provisions they could. The three wounded

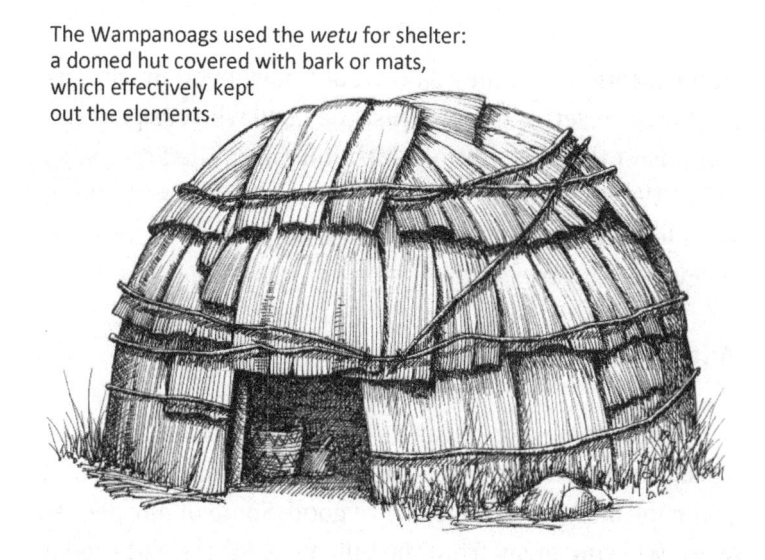

The Wampanoags used the *wetu* for shelter: a domed hut covered with bark or mats, which effectively kept out the elements.

Indian men were brought back to our village. After their wounds were dressed and cared for, they returned home.

After all this, many Indian chiefs congratulated us and our peace with them was strengthened. Even those from Capawock Island came to befriend us. Corbitant himself had Massasoit mediate a peace between us and him, but for a long time after that he never came near.

On the 18th of September, Squanto guided ten of our men to search the bay and establish trade with the natives. Not only were they successful, but they were greeted with warm hospitality all along the way. They also learned that many of the natives were afraid of the Tarrantines to the east. These Indians would arrive at harvest time to demand the corn of the other tribes, even killing them to get what they wanted.

Our party safely returned with many beaver skins and gave us a good report about the area. They found another location that they said would have been much better for us to settle, but we trust the Lord who assigns "the bounds of their habitation" for all men, as the Scriptures say.[21] We found that the Lord is always with us in all we do, blessing our journeys. Let his holy name be praised forever and ever.

Autumn and a Good Harvest

When fall came, we began to harvest our food and prepare our homes for winter. Our strength and health had returned and our supplies were good. Some of our people were working away from the village as others gathered a great supply of cod, bass, and other fish. Every family had plenty. Throughout the entire summer there was no lack of food.

With winter approaching we began harvesting fowl, which were great in number when we first arrived but had decreased some since then. We brought in ducks, many wild turkeys, deer, and other game, along with a great supply of Indian corn. From the beginning of our harvest there was such an abundance of food each week for everyone. Of all the letters we had written to our friends in England about our great food supply, none of them were overstated, but they were all completely true.

---

[21] Acts 17:6.

[Dear reader: In his booklet, *Mourt's Relation*, the early Pilgrim leader Edward Winslow records a historical event that occurred at this time within Plymouth colony. I include this in William Bradford's journal because of its historical significance, for here Mr. Winslow describes what we now call the "First Thanksgiving." - D.W.]

In the short time we have been here we have built seven homes and also four structures for the use of all on the plantation. We are now preparing to build more. Last spring we planted twenty acres of Indian corn and six acres of barley and peas. We fertilized our seed in the Indian manner using fish, which we have in great abundance and are easily obtained from the brook that runs just alongside our settlement. God be praised, we had a great harvest of Indian corn. Some of the barley came up, but our peas were not worth harvesting. We think we planted them late because they started to blossom, but then withered in the sun.

Our crops were all gathered in when our governor sent four men out to hunt fowl for a special celebration to rejoice over our wonderful harvest. Those men killed so many fowl that, with some other provisions, it fed our people for nearly a week. Along with other entertainment, we practiced shooting our muskets. The great chief Massasoit, along with ninety of his men, joined us for our celebration, feasting with us for three days. His men went out and killed five deer and brought them back to our governor, the captain, and the others. And though it is not always this plentiful for us, by the goodness of God we are so far from need that we wish you were here to share our abundance.

In November, about one year after we arrived, we were astonished at the arrival of a small English ship. Thirty-six people came off of the *Fortune*, and with them was our friend Robert Cushman. Except for him, all of them came over to join our settlement, and we were very glad. And when the new settlers came ashore and saw how much food and provisions there were in every house, they were greatly relieved. For most of them were healthy, spirited, restless young men who had no care in the world, but when they first sailed into the lifeless harbor of Cape Cod, they saw nothing but desolate shore.

When the new settlers first caught a glimpse of the empty harbor and could not see any trace of a settlement, they started worrying about their own fate. They wondered if we all had died or were killed by Indians.

As they approached the shore, some of the new arrivals overheard the sailors murmuring, leading them to suspect that they were all about to be helplessly abandoned to a mercilessness land—so they devised a plan. If they saw no signs of an English settlement, they would forcibly take over the ship. The captain, however, learned of their plot. He gave them his word that if something tragic had truly happened to our people, he would not leave them there in a lifeless harbor, but instead he would take them south to the safety of the Virginia settlement. He further promised that if his crew had any extra food, they would share it with them for the remainder of the voyage. Upon hearing this, they were all relieved.

When they finally came ashore, not one person brought along any food—not even a biscuit. Nor did they have any bedding. Some brought a few pitiful things, but no pots, no pans, and very little in clothing, explaining to us that they had got rid of their coats and cloaks in England before they sailed. They did, however, bring a few simple suits from Birching Lane in London. We were glad to have more people, but we couldn't fathom why they were all so frightfully ill-prepared. Yet that could not be helped now.

We loaded the *Fortune* with as much good clapboard siding as she could carry, along with two barrels of beaver and otter skins. We all agreed that we should quickly gather a supply of goods to return to Thomas Weston and the investors, according to the agreement that we all signed one year before. We estimated that the freight we sent back was worth nearly 500 English pounds. All this we traded in return for a few trifling supplies from the crew; they were so unprepared for any trade. Not one of the crew had ever seen a beaver skin before until Squanto had showed them upon their arrival.

Mr. Cushman brought a letter from Mr. Weston. In it he complained about all the extra months we kept the *Mayflower*, the additional cost that it created for his investors, and that we had sent the ship back without any goods to sell. The *Fortune* soon sailed away, and Mr. Cushman went back with it, for Mr. Weston and the company had merely sent him to inspect our plantation and check on their investment.

Mr. Weston proved unreliable to us. He had initially

promised that even if all other investors stopped supporting our endeavor that he himself would never back out, but would stick with us so long as we load the ship with goods. But all his words were merely wind, for we later heard that he was the first and only man who left the agreement—even before the *Mayflower* had returned.

So vain is confidence in man. But I will write more about this in its time.

[Dear reader: Governor Bradford inserted this following note into chapter five many years later. Therefore, as a much older man, these were William Bradford's later reflections on what became of Plymouth Colony. - D.W.]

> *Oh, sacred bond which is faithfully preserved, how sweet and precious were its fruits! But when this faithfulness decayed, then their ruin approached. Oh, that these ancient members had not died, if only God allowed, or if only this holy care and constant faithfulness had still remained with those that survived. But, alas, that stealthy serpent has slyly wound himself to untwist these sacred bonds and ties. In my earlier days I was happy to see and enjoy the blessed fruits of that sweet communion, but it is now a misery in my old age that I feel its decay and lament it, grieving in my heart.*
>
> *For the warning and admonition of others, and for my own humiliation, I here make note of it.*

QUESTIONS FOR REFLECTION AND DISCUSSION:

1. The *Mayflower* and crew remained at Cape Cod for nearly five months. Why did they stay much longer than they originally planned?

2. In what ways did Squanto help the Pilgrims? How might the story of the Plymouth colony turn out different without the help of Samoset and Squanto?

3. Considering all the sickness, death, and hardship those first several months, why did the Pilgrims choose to stay instead of returning to England? What kinds of personal qualities would it take to make such a choice?

4. What happened to young John Billington? How did his experience end up helping the Pilgrim community?

5. Why were Hobomok and Squanto threatened? What do you think about the Pilgrim's response to Squanto's capture?

6. What may have surprised you about the event we now call the "First Thanksgiving"? What elements of it seemed familiar to you?

7. Describe the thoughts and feelings of the passengers aboard the *Fortune* as they approached Cape Cod. From what Bradford says, how were the new settlers both a blessing and a burden to the Plymouth colony?

APPENDIX 1

THIS IS A WRITTEN SERMON that Governor Bradford later inserted into chapter one regarding what he sees as God's victory over the authorities of the Church of England, whom he believes are far too similar to the Catholic Church (or "popery," as he calls it). I have left the many biblical references within the text, just as Bradford had done in his original writing.

This is a later observation, as it were by the way, worthy to be noted:

Little did I think that the downfall of the Bishops—with their courts, creeds, and ceremonies—was so near when I first began scribbling these writings (which was about 1630), with bits and pieces written later at different times. Nor did I think I would ever live to see or hear of their downfall, but "this is the Lord's doing" and it ought to be "marvelous in our eyes!" (Psalm 118:23). "Every plant which my Heavenly Father has not planted," says our Savior, "shall be rooted up" (Matt. 15:13). "I have snared you, and you are taken, O Babel," symbolizing the church Bishops, "and you were not aware. You are found and also caught, because you have fought against the Lord" (Jer. 50:24).

But must they fight against the truth, against the servants of God, against even the Lord himself? "Do they provoke the Lord to anger? Are they stronger than he?" (1Cor. 10:22) No, no! They have met their match. "Behold, I come to you, O proud man, says the Lord God of Hosts, for your day is come, even the time that I will visit you" (Jer. 50:31). May not the people of God—including our own humble people—now say, "The Lord has brought forth our righteousness! Come, let us declare in Zion the work of the Lord our God" (Jer. 51:10)? "Let all flesh be still before the Lord; for he is raised up out of his holy place" (Zech. 2:13).

In these events, our own humble people today may declare, along with the thousands from ancient Israel, "When the Lord brought back the captives to Zion, we were like them that dream" (Psalm 126:1). "The Lord has done great things for us, therefore we rejoice" (Psalm 126:3). "They that sow in tears, shall reap in joy. They went weeping, and carried precious seed, but they shall return with joy and bring their sheaves" (Psalm 126:5-6).

Do you not now see the fruits of your labors, all you servants of the Lord who have suffered for his truth? All you who have been faithful witnesses of the truth, though you are only a handful among the rest, the least among the thousands of Israel (Micah 5:2), you have not only planted seeds, but many of you have seen the joyful harvest. Should you not then rejoice, yes and again rejoice

(Phil. 4:4), and say, "Hallelujah! Salvation and glory and honor and power be to the Lord our God; for true and righteous are his judgments" (Rev. 19:1-2)?

But you will ask, "What is the matter? What happened?" Are you a stranger in Israel that you should not know what happened (Luke 24:18)? Have not these church officials been overcome, just like the Jebusites who troubled the people of Israel for so long, who even ruled Jerusalem until the days of King David? They were thorns in the sides of Israel for ages, and those who follow their footsteps today now protest against anyone like David meddling with them. They began to fortify their tower, like the Babylonians of old, but these prideful authorities are thrown down like the pagan Anakites, and their glory is laid in the dust.

The tyrannous bishops are ejected, their courts dissolved, their laws forceless, their service dismissed, their ceremonies useless and despised, their plots for popery prevented, and all their superstitions discarded and returned to Rome from where they came, and the monuments of idolatry are driven out of the land. And those proud and profane supporters and cruel defenders of these practices (such as bloody papists, wicked atheists, and their malignant consorts) are all marvelously overthrown. And are these things not great? Who can deny it?

And who has done all this? Who else, but "he that sits on the white horse, who is called Faithful and True, and judges and fights righteously" (Rev. 19:11), whose "garments are dipped in blood, and his name was called the Word of God" (Rev. 19:13). For "he shall rule them with a rod of iron; for it is he that treads the winepress of the fierceness and wrath of God Almighty. And he has upon his garment and thigh a name written—the King of Kings and Lord of Lords" (Rev. 19:15-16).

Hallelujah!

APPENDIX 2

102 MAYFLOWER PASSENGERS LISTED ACCORDING TO FAMILIES:

UPPERCASE = those who were members of the church in Leiden, Holland.

* = those who died before November 11, 1621 (within one year after the *Mayflower* landed).

Alden, John (b. 1599? d. Sept. 12, 1687)

ALLERTON, Isaac (b. 1586? d. Feb. 1658 or 59)
* ALLERTON, Mary (Norris) - wife of Isaac
    (b. 1590? d. Feb. 25, 1621)
ALLERTON, Bartholomew - son (b. 1612? d. 1658 - 59?)
ALLERTON, Mary - daughter (b. 1616? d. Nov. 28, 1699)
ALLERTON, Remember - daughter (b. 1614? d. 1652 - 56?)

* Allerton, John - no known relation to Isaac
    (b.? d. by Apr. 10, 1621)

Billington, John (b. 1590? d. Sept. 1630)
Billington, Eleanor - wife of John
    (b. 1580? d. after Mar. 12, 1642 or 43)
Billington, John - son (b. 1604? d. 1627 - 30)
Billington, Francis - son (b. 1606 - 09? d. Dec. 3, 1684)

BRADFORD, William (b. 1589 - 90? d. May 9, 1657)
* BRADFORD, Dorothy (May) - wife of William
    (b. 1597? d. Dec. 7, 1620)

BREWSTER, William (b. 1566 - 67? d. Apr. 10, 1644)
BREWSTER, Mary - wife of William
    (b. 1668 - 69? d. Apr. 17, 1627)
BREWSTER, Love - son (b. 1611, d. by Jan. 31, 1650)
BREWSTER, Wrestling - son (b. 1614, d. 1635)

* Britteridge, Richard (b.? - Dec. 21, 1620)

Browne, Peter (b. before 1600, d. 1633)

* Button, William (b. 1598, d. at sea, Nov. 6, 1620)

* Carter, Robert (b.? d. winter of 1620 - 21)

* CARVER, John (b. 1565, d. soon after Apr. 5, 1621).
* CARVER, Katherine (White) - wife of John
    (b. 1580, d. May or June, 1621)
* CHILTON, James (b. 1556? d. Dec. 8, 1620)
* CHILTON, Mrs. - wife of James (b.? d. early 1621).
CHILTON, Mary - daughter (b. 1607? d. before May 1, 1679)

* Clarke, Richard (b. 1604? d. winter of 1620 - 21)

COOKE, Francis (b. 1583? d. Apr. 7, 1663)
COOKE, John - son (b. 1606? d. Nov. 23, 1695)

COOPER, Humility (b. 1612, d. 1639 - 51)

* CRACKSTON, John (b. 1575? d. Jan. - Mar. 1621)
CRACKSTON, John - son (b.? d. 1627 - 28)

Doty, Edward (b. before 1600? d. Aug. 23, 1655)

Eaton, Francis (b. 1595 - 96? d. fall 1633)
* Eaton, Sarah - wife of Francis (b.? d. winter of 1620 - 21)
Eaton, Samuel - son (b. 1620, d. 1684?)

* English, Thomas (b. 1595? d. winter of 1620 - 21)

* FLETCHER, Moses (b. 1564? d. winter of 1620 - 21)

* FULLER, Edward (b. 1575? d. winter of 1620 - 21)
* FULLER, ? - wife of Edward (b.? d. Jan. 1621)
FULLER, Samuel - son (b. 1608? d. Oct. 31, 1683)

FULLER, Samuel - brother of Edward
     (b. 1579? d. late summer 1633)

Gardinar, Richard (b. 1582? d. before 1651)

* GOODMAN, John (b. 1595? d. winter of 1620 - 21?)

* Holbeck, William (b. after 1599, d. winter of 1620 - 21)

* Hooke, John (b. 1607? d. winter of 1620 - 21)

Hopkins, Stephen (b. 1576? d. June - July, 1644)
Hopkins, Elizabeth (Fisher) - wife of Stephen
     (b. 1585? d. 1638 - 44)
Hopkins, Giles - son (b. Jan. 30, 1607 - 08? d. 1688 - 90)
Hopkins, Constance - daughter (b. 1606? d. Oct. 1677)
Hopkins, Damaris - daughter (b. 1618? d. by 1627)
Hopkins, Oceanus - son (born at sea: fall 1620, d. by 1627)
Howland, John (b. 1592 - 99? d. Feb. 23, 1672 or 73)

* Langmore, John (b. after 1599, d. winter of 1620 - 21)

Latham, William (b. 1609? d. 1645 - 51)

Leister, Edward (b. 1595 - 99? d. 1623 - 51?)

Margesson, Edmund (b.? d. winter of 1620 - 21)

* Martin, Christopher (b. 1582? d. January 8, 1621)
* Martin, Mary (Prower) - wife of Christopher
         (b.? d. winter of 1620 - 21)

MINTER, Desire (b. 1618? d. by 1650)

* More, Ellen - sister (b. 1612? d. winter of 1620 - 21)
* More, Jasper - brother (b. 1613? d. Dec. 6, 1620)
  More, Richard - brother (b. 1614? d. late 1690s?)
* More, Mary - sister (b. 1616? d. winter of 1620 - 21)

* Mullins, William (b. 1572? d. Feb. 21, 1621)
* Mullins, Alice - wife of William (b. 1575? d. early 1621)
  Mullins, Priscilla - daughter (b. 1602? d. 1651 - 87)
* Mullins, Joseph - son (b. 1596? d. winter of 1620 - 21)

PRIEST, Degory (b. 1580? d. Jan. 1, 1621)

* Prower, Solomon (b. by 1604, d. Dec. 24, 1620)

* Rigsdale, John (b.? d. winter of 1620 - 21)
* Rigsdale, Alice - wife of John (b.? d. winter of 1620 - 21)

* ROGERS, Thomas (b. 1572? d. winter of 1620 - 21)
  ROGERS, Joseph - son (b. 1602 - 03? d. Jan. 2, 1677 or 78)

SAMSON, Henry (b. 1603 or 04, d. Dec. 24, 1684)

Soule, George (b. 1595 - 99? d. 1677 - 80)

Standish, Myles (b. 1593? d. Oct. 3, 1656)

Standish, Rose - wife of Myles (b.? d. winter of 1620 - 21)

* Story, Elias (b. after 1599? d. winter of 1620 - 21)
* Thompson, Edward (b.? d. Dec. 4, 1620)

A PLYMOUTH PILGRIM

* TILLEY, Edward (b. 1588? d. winter of 1620 - 21)
* TILLEY, Agnes (Cooper) - wife of Edward
     (b. 1585? d. winter of 1620 - 21)

* TILLEY, John - brother to Edward
     (b. 1571? d. winter of 1620 - 21)
* TILLEY, Joan (Hurst) - wife of John
     (b. 1567 - 68? d. winter of 1620 - 21)
  TILLEY, Elizabeth - daughter (b. 1607? d. Dec. 22, 1687)

* Tinker, Thomas (b.? d. winter of 1620 - 21)
* Tinker, ? - wife of Thomas (b.? d. winter of 1620 - 21)
* Tinker, ? - son (b.? d. winter of 1620 - 21)

* TURNER, John (b. 1590? d. winter of 1620 - 21)
* TURNER, ? - son (b.? d. winter of 1620 - 21)
* TURNER, ? - son (b.? d. winter of 1620 - 21)

  Warren, Richard (b. 1578? d. 1628)

* White, William (b. 1590? d. Feb. 21, 1620)
  White, Susanna - wife of William (b. 1590? d. 1654 - 75?)
  White, Resolved - son (b. 1615? d. after Sept. 19, 1687)

* Wilder, Roger (b. after 1599? d. winter of 1620 - 21)

* Williams, Thomas (b. Aug. 12, 1982, d. winter of 1620 - 21)

  WINSLOW, Edward (b. Oct. 18, 1595, d. May 8, 1655)
* WINSLOW, Elizabeth (Barker) - wife of Edward
     (b. 1597? d. March 24, 1621)

  Winslow, Gilbert - brother to Edward (b. 1600? d. 1631?)

  Unnamed female servant (b.? d. 1624?)

APPENDIX 3

TIMELINE OF SIGNIFICANT EVENTS LEADING UP TO THE FOUNDING OF PLYMOUTH PLANTATION

1382

John Wycliffe, an English theologian, completes the first English translation of the Bible. His translation work, and his teachings against Catholic practices and doctrine, fuel the passions of early church reformers.

1455

Johannes Gutenberg finishes printing the entire Bible (in Latin) using his invention of a printing press with movable type, giving people far wider access to literature and knowledge by mass-producing the printed page.

1492

Columbus lands in the Bahamas and Cuba, just south of the North American continent, opening up the Americas for European commerce, conflict, and colonization.

1521
Martin Luther, a Catholic priest, is expelled from the Roman Catholic Church, which begins a Christian movement (Protestantism) which protests against the authority of the Pope and the Catholic Priesthood.

1522
Martin Luther publishes his German translation of the New Testament, the first major Bible publication to be used for the common person, opening the door for ordinary citizens to read and evaluate the teachings of the Bible for themselves.

1526
William Tyndale's English translation of the entire New Testament is printed in Germany.

1534
England's King Henry VIII declares himself the head of the "Church of England," pulling the English church away from the authority (not the doctrine) of the Pope and the Roman Catholic Church.

1535
Myles Coverdale publishes his Bible—the first complete Bible printed in English.

1539

The Great Bible is published—the first English language Bible authorized by the English government for public use. Copies were first placed in churches to allow the public access to it. To discourage religious controversy, King Henry VIII prohibited any marginal notes in the text. Soon afterwards the King bans all other English translations of the Bible.

1543

The English Government prohibits most of the public (generally common laborers) from access to the Bible.

1553

Queen Mary I inherits the throne and returns England to Catholicism, persecuting the Protestant church leaders. Nearly 300 Protestant Christians are burned at the stake, earning her the nickname of "Bloody Mary." Hundreds of English Protestants flee to the safety of Europe, establishing churches in nations such as Holland, Germany, and Switzerland.

1558

Mary I dies and Elizabeth I becomes Queen of England, leading the nation into a final break from the authority of the Catholic Church.

1560

The entire Geneva Bible is published, which is an English translation that includes extensive notes from Protestant church scholars throughout the text.

1560s

Many Protestants demand that the Church of England become even more radically purified from the historical Catholic influences upon their doctrine and practice. These people are labeled "Puritans" by those who consider their beliefs and demands too extreme.

1563

John Foxe publishes his *Book of Martyrs* in English, detailing the history of the persecution of Protestant Christians at the hands of Catholic authorities, focusing especially on Great Britain.

1581

Robert Browne, a Puritan-trained church scholar, leaves England to begin a church in the Netherlands. His followers (called "Brownists") become a Separatist movement, believing it is best to separate from the Church of England and establish their own congregations.

1607

English authorities arrest Separatist church members meeting at the home of William Brewster in Scrooby village. The teenage William Bradford was a member of this church at the time. Jamestown, the first permanent English settlement in America, is founded in the Virginia territory near the mouth of the Chesapeake Bay.

1608

William Brewster and others from the church in Scrooby flee to Holland for religious freedom. They settle in Leiden, and are led by Pastor John Robinson.

1611

The King James Bible is published in England in part to discourage the use of other English translations (e.g., the Geneva Bible) that were deemed a threat to the authority of the Church of England and the English Monarchy.

1614

Thomas Hunt, an English ship captain, kidnaps twenty-four Wampanoag natives from Patuxet village (later called "Plymouth") to sell as slaves in Spain. One of them was a young man named Tisquantum (or "Squanto"), who finds his way to London to live and work with shipbuilder and merchant John Slany.

1616

English explorer John Smith publishes *Descriptions of New England*, a book on his adventures in the American Northeast coastal regions. William Brewster will later take this book with him on the *Mayflower*.

1619

Squanto, now fluent in English, finally returns to his homeland only to find the entire Patuxet village wiped out by disease carried in by Europeans. He finds a home with Chief Massasoit and his people. Two years later he would serve as mentor, translator, and friend to the English colony in Plymouth.

1620

102 English settlers voyage across the Atlantic on the *Mayflower* to make a home in New England. Among them are thirty-seven Separatists from Leiden, Holland.

APPENDIX 4

THE FOLLOWING TEXT is the introduction and first section of chapter one, just as William Bradford wrote it, with his original words, spelling, and punctuation. See how well you can read and understand Bradford's 400-year-old English.

Of Plimoth Plantation.

And first of ye occasion and indusments ther unto; the which that I may truly unfould, I must begine at ye very roote & rise of ye same. The which I shall endevor to manefest in a plaine stile, with singuler regard unto ye simple trueth in all things, at least as near as my slender judgmente can attaine the same.

1. Chapter.

It is well knowne unto ye godly and judicious, how ever since ye first breaking out of ye lighte of ye gospel in our Honourable Nation of England, (which was ye first of nations whom ye Lord adorned ther with, affter yt grosse darknes of popery which had covered & overspred ye Christian worled,) what warrs & opposissions ever since, Satan hath raised, maintained, and continued against the Sainctes, from time to time, in one sorte or other. Some times by bloody death and cruell torments; other whiles imprisonments, banishments, & other hard usages; as being loath his kingdom should goe downe, the trueth prevaile, and ye churches of God reverte to their anciente puritie, and recover their primative order, libertie, & bewtie. But when he could not prevaile by these means, against the maine trueths of ye gospell, but that they began to take rootting in many places, being watered with ye blooud of ye martires, and blessed from heaven with a gracious encrease; He then begane to take him to his anciente strategemes, used of old against the first Christians. That when by ye bloody & barbarous persecutions of ye Heathen Emperours, he could not stoppe & subuerte the course of ye gospell, but that it speedily overspred with a wounderfull celeritie the then best known parts of ye world, He then begane to sow errours, heresies, and wounderfull dissentions amongst ye professours them selves, (working upon their pride & ambition, with other corrupte passions incidente to all mortall men, yea to ye saints them selves in some measure,) by which wofull effects followed; as not only bitter contentions, & hartburnings, schismes, with other horrible confusions, but Satan tooke occasion & advantage therby to foyst in a number of vile ceremoneys, with many unproffitable cannons & decrees, which have since been as snares to many poore & peaceable souls even to this day. So as in ye anciente times, the persecutions by ye heathen & their Emperours, was not greater then of the Christians one against other; the Arians & other their complices against ye orthodoxe & true Christians. As witneseth Socrates in his 2. books. His words are these; The violence truly (saith he) was no less than that of ould practised towards ye Christians when they were compelled & drawne to sacrifice to idoles; for many indured sundrie kinds of tormente, often rackings, & dismembering of their joynts; confiscating of ther goods some bereaved of their native soyle; others departed this life under ye hands of ye tormentor; and some died in banishmete, & never saw ther cuntrie againe, &c. The like methode Satan hath seemed to hold in these later times since ye trueth begane to springe & spread after ye great defection made by Antichrist, yt man of sine.

RECOMMENDED RESOURCES

BOOKS:

Bradford, William, *Of Plymouth Plantation*, (several editions are available).

Bragdon, Kathleen, *Native People of Southern New England, 1500-1650* (1996).

Bunker, Nick, *Making Haste from Babylon: The Mayflower Pilgrims and Their World: A New History* (2010).

Calloway, Colin, *New Worlds for All: Indians, Europeans, and the Remaking of Early America* (1997).

Deetz, James and Patricia, *The Times of Their Lives: Life, Love, and Death in Plymouth Colony* (2000).

Hawke, David, *Everyday Life in Early America* (1989).

Lense, James, *Preceding the Mayflower: The Pilgrims in England and in the Netherlands* (1972)

Philbrick, Nathaniel, *Mayflower: A Story of Courage, Community, and War* (2006).

Segal, Charles and David Stineback, *Puritans, Indians, and Manifest Destiny* (1977).

INTERNET:

Plimoth Plantation Living Museum
plimoth.org

Pilgrim Hall Museum
pilgrimhallmuseum.org

Caleb Johnson, Mayflower Historian
mayflowerhistory.com

Sue Allen, Scrooby Village Historian
mayflowermaid.com

Wampanoag People of Cape Cod
mashpeewampanoagtribe.com

General Society of Mayflower Descendants
themayflowersociety.org

Made in the USA
Monee, IL
08 November 2025